0004277

D1448239

20431

UNF

URBAN AND REGIO...
EMPLOYMENT CHANGE IN
THE UK

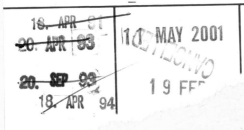

This book is to be returned on or before
the last date stamped below.

18. APR 01

20. APR 93   1(MAY 2001

20. SEP 93   19 FF

18. APR 94

B 6652

UNEQUAL GROWTH
URBAN AND REGIONAL EMPLOYMENT CHANGE IN THE UK

Stephen Fothergill
and
Graham Gudgin

 Heinemann Educational Books

To Steve's parents and to Graham's children, David and Emma

Heinemann Educational Books Ltd
22, Bedford Square, London WCIB 3HH.
LONDON EDINBURGH MELBOURNE AUCKLAND
TORONTO HONG KONG SINGAPORE KUALA LUMPUR
NEW DELHI NAIROBI JOHANNESBURG IBADAN
KINGSTON

© Stephen Fothergill and Graham Gudgin 1982
First Published 1982

British Library Cataloguing in Publication Data
Fothergill, Stephen
  Unequal growth.
  1. Labor Supply—Great Britain
  2. Great Britain—Industries
  I. Title   II. Gudgin, Graham
  331. 11′1′ 0941   HD 5765.A6

ISBN 0 435 843702 (Cased)
ISBN 0 435 84371 0 (Paper)

SB 20431 6 50 483

Photosetting by Thomson Press (India) Limited,
New Delhi, India
Printed by Biddles Ltd, Guildford, Surrey.

Contents

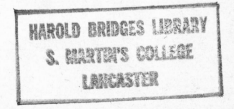

HAROLD BRIDGES LIBRARY
S. MARTIN'S COLLEGE
LANCASTER

List of Tables and Figures

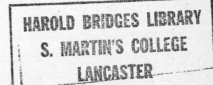
HAROLD BRIDGES LIBRARY
S. MARTIN'S COLLEGE
LANCASTER

Preface

The publication of this book comes at a time when more and more people are becoming worried by urban and regional employment trends—and with good reason. As the national economy deteriorates, the deep-seated economic weakness in much of northern and western Britain and in inner city areas ensures that these places inevitably take the brunt of the decline. In some depressed areas unemployment is already approaching levels hitherto reached only in the 1930s.

The causes of the decline in the British economy are hotly debated—and seem likely to remain so—but it is remarkable how little is understood about the causes of the problems in depressed regions. This is true despite a large academic literature, and despite the fact that current problems have been evident, with varying degrees of severity, for over half a century. Why does employment in some areas remain buoyant even during recessions? Why do other areas decline despite massive aid? And why are large cities experiencing such dramatic job losses?

These are important questions to which this book provides some answers. It presents the findings of a research project which began in 1976 at the Centre for Environmental Studies (CES), an independent research institute based in London, though some of the ideas have roots in our earlier research on company formation and growth (Gudgin, 1978) and on sub-regional employment trends. The project was funded mainly by the Department of the Environment (DoE), and also by a smaller grant from the Social Science Research Council which financed some of the work on new firms. As social science research projects go it was quite expensive, costing around £100,000 over four years. It is up to the reader to judge whether the findings of the study were worth this amount of public money but we should point out that under present government policy the work would probably not have been financed. Indeed, the withdrawal of public funds from CES, forcing its closure, was one of the first acts of a new government anxious to cut what in its view was inessential public expenditure. On a more general point, the low priority currently attached to social and economic research is worrying because public policies in many fields are unlikely to be successful or cost-effective unless they are based upon a sound understanding of the problems to which they are addressed. In the context of the expenditure of several hundred million pounds a year on regional economic policy, and in the light of the existing muddled understanding of urban and regional growth, continued spending on research ought to be regarded as a sensible investment.

There are a great many people to whom we owe thanks for helping to bring this work to fruition. Perhaps we should start by mentioning Bob Howard and David Keeble, who acted as external advisers to the project and provided wonderfully detailed comments on the first draft of the book. Colin Bishop deserves thanks as our DoE link-person. Other researchers helped us enormously both through their own work, which has often guided ours, and by providing practical assistance and data. Barry Moore, John Rhodes, Peter Tyler, Ross MacKay, David Storey, and Peter Lloyd deserve special mention. Brian McLeish, Peter Willmott and Jill Vincent assisted in re-drafting the text, and Jill also deserves thanks for acting as our landlady when we undertook survey work. The Departments of Industry and Employment, the Health and Safety Executive, and Industrial Market Location Ltd. provided data without which this study would not have been possible. And we are very grateful to the managers of the firms who spared some of their time to talk to us.

But most of all we are indebted to those who worked alongside us at various times during the four years it took to complete this study. Sigrid Grieg Gran, Ceinwen Sanderson and Melanie Hare provided secretarial assistance, and never complained when faced with voluminous quantities of typing. Irene Brunskill joined us as a researcher during the latter stages of the project, and made an important contribution to our work on new firms and on company profitability. Our thanks also to Ibrahim Boolaky, Jane Clifford, Jorge Fiori, Tom Hazard, Sally McKean, Mick Morrissey, Bryan Reed and Kathy Sutton, who all worked with us as research assistants at one time or another. Of these, three deserve a special mention: Mick, who worked wonders on the computer during his college holidays, and Sally and Kathy, whose sustained hard work saw us through a particularly tedious stage of the research. This book bears our names as authors, but it is the fruits of their labour as well as our own.

Finally, a brief word on three conventions we have used throughout the book. Firstly, unless otherwise stated all tables and figures are based on statistics compiled or adapted by ourselves.

Secondly, for the sake of convenience we refer to Scotland, Wales and Northern Ireland as 'regions', but no affront to nationalist sentiments is intended. Thirdly, to maintain readability we include references to the work of others only when this is absolutely necessary in order to develop our argument on any one point. The scarcity of references should not therefore be taken to imply any disregard for, or unawareness of, some of the excellent research which has been undertaken in the past.

Stephen Fothergill
Graham Gudgin
Cambridge
1981

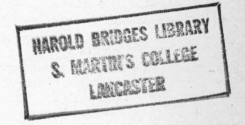

HAROLD BRIDGES LIBRARY
S. MARTIN'S COLLEGE
LANCASTER

1 Introduction

In an industrial economy the growth of cities and regions depends first and foremost on the growth of the national economy. During the post-war period the performance of the British economy has been poor, and over the last decade the deterioration has become particularly serious. At first the problem was that living standards were rising at only half the rate of those of most other Western economies, but more recently production has stagnated while unemployment has risen to levels approaching those of the 1930s, an era which most people thought had vanished forever.

Within this depressing context all parts of the country have shared in the relatively slow rise in living standards, and unemployment has increased everywhere. But in other respects the experience of different areas has been profoundly unequal. East Anglia, for example, is one of the fastest growing regions in Europe, and the South West has done quite well too, but at the other end of the scale some areas, such as London and parts of northern England, have lost people and jobs at an unprecedented rate. The causes of these inequalities in employment growth form the subject matter of this book, but before setting out to describe and account for them it is important to state clearly why they matter.

The main reason is that there is no mechanism which automatically matches the supply of jobs to the supply of workers. In theory, if wages were flexible and fell when job shortages occurred, production costs would fall in an area with a job shortage and thus allow firms in that area to lower their prices and compete more effectively. This in turn would lead to an increase in the number of jobs, thereby removing the labour surplus through the operation of market forces. However, it is a deeply embedded and cherished feature of British economic life that wages do not fluctuate in the face of supply and demand but instead reflect comparability between occupations. This feature is maintained through national wage bargaining, so that regional differences in wages do not reflect local labour market conditions. Wage adjustments therefore fail to guide jobs into the areas where the shortages are most acute, and companies and organisations alter employment levels in ways which bear little relationship to local needs. In some areas the demand for labour outstrips local supply and migrants are attracted from elsewhere. In others the demand for labour fails to match supply and the result is a combination of rising unemployment and out-migration.

In places where the indigenous labour force exceeds the number of jobs available it is still possible for most people to find satisfactory jobs. Of those who cannot, some may decide to stay in their home area and accept lesser jobs while others may migrate to another part of the country or go abroad to seek suitable employment. But if migration fails to reduce the size of the labour force to the point where it matches the number of jobs it is inevitable that some people will become registered as unemployed and others, especially women, will drop out of the labour market altogether.

The evidence of the recent past (Cambridge Economic Policy Group 1980b) is that large numbers of people *do* migrate out of areas experiencing job shortages and into areas where jobs are more plentiful. Migration reduces levels of unemployment in depressed areas, but adds to the dole queue in more prosperous regions because in-migrants take some of the jobs which would otherwise have gone to local residents. This is the main reason why the disparities in unemployment rates between growing and declining areas are not a great deal wider, and also why in recent years unemployment has risen even in those regions (such as East Anglia) where employment has expanded quite rapidly.

The full equalisation of unemployment rates, via migration, is prevented by a number of factors which inhibit mobility. Some people have strong family ties and other attachments in their localities which mean that unemployment, either temporary or permanent, is preferred to migration. Older and unskilled workers find it difficult to compete for jobs anywhere and are consequently relatively immobile. People in these categories who become unemployed in areas of job shortages often find it impossible to move and thereby maintain or increase disparities in unemployment between different parts of the country. Housing problems exacerbate this immobility. Long-distance moves within the council house sector are extremely difficult, in the owner-occupied sector the higher level of house prices in prosperous regions effectively rules out many moves, and the privately rented sector, which might have acted as a useful channel for migration, has now all but disappeared.

High rates of registered unemployment, low rates of participation in the labour force and out-migration are all symptoms of the same underlying problem: a shortage of jobs. Generally, the incidence of the shortage mirrors the uneven growth and decline of employment, though this is not the whole story. In Northern Ireland in particular, and in Scotland to a lesser extent, the shortage of jobs is at least in part due to above-average birth rates—leading to relatively high rates of natural increase in the local workforce—which means that employment in these regions must increase faster than elsewhere if the problems of rising unemployment and out-migration are to be avoided. But whatever the cause of the shortages, the fact remains that the inequality in employment opportunities between different parts of Britain is widely recognised as a serious social and economic problem. Moreover, policies designed to balance local and regional labour markets by reducing the birth rate in places such as Northern Ireland and Scotland are clearly not realistic options, and in any case would take decades to have much effect, and so the emphasis must be on the growth of employment itself. The main aim must be to alter the pattern of unequal growth in order to bring about a fairer distribution of jobs.

Approaches to the Problem

Public policy is more likely to achieve this goal if it is based on a sound understanding of the causes of unequal growth in employment, and in the chapters which follow we therefore set out to explain why some parts of Britain experience growth while others decline. By taking a long view, and by examining employment changes in considerable detail where necessary, it is possible to assemble evidence on the different factors which bring about growth and decline, how they vary from one region to another, and how they alter in importance through time. The persistence and strength of some influences suggest that certain conclusions can be generalised over much longer periods than that which we have investigated. Also, with the aid of supporting evidence from other countries, we can tentatively extend some of our main conclusions beyond Britain to other Western industrial economies.

The forces which determine urban and regional employment change have hitherto not been properly understood. On some occasions the problem in declining areas is ascribed to 'old' industries, and on others to firms 'moving out'. Some blame the unions; others blame the multinationals. The confusion has meant that successive governments have attempted to tackle the shortage of jobs in depressed areas without knowing why employment grows in some places but not in others, and their policies have therefore rarely addressed the underlying problems. Although this approach has not been entirely without success, traditional regional policies have certainly not lived up to initial expectations and their shortcomings are now becoming painfully obvious. Twenty years of active policy have done little to narrow regional imbalances in employment opportunities, and have still not provided the basis for self-sustaining growth in the assisted areas. In spite of these failings, governments have so far been unwilling to strengthen the existing tools of regional policy sufficiently for them to be really effective. Greater public direction of private investment has not been acceptable, nor a drastic increase in the already generous grants and subsidies available in assisted areas. The growing awareness of economic decline in inner city areas poses still further problems for government policy because there is even less consensus about how to tackle urban decline than about the solutions to long-standing regional problems.

In this situation academic research ought to present a clear analysis of the nature of the problems and the possible ways out of the present impasse, but it is often confused and misleading. For example, despite the rapid decline of industry in cities and its growth in small towns and rural areas, which has been going on for at least twenty years, it is still possible to read discussions of the 'agglomeration economies' which are supposed to advantage large cities. Also, despite the manifest inflexibility in wages, many textbooks retain the idea that regional employment problems will be self-correcting because labour surpluses will depress wages and improve an area's competitiveness. The irrelevance of these ideas is clear from the way they assume away the very problems we need to understand: they describe unreal worlds in which permanently high regional unemployment or urban decline would not arise.

Two other groups of respectable academic theories do not help much either. One is the body of classical industrial location theory. This concerns itself with the interaction between profit-maximising firms and an environment in which costs of production and distribution vary from place to place, and argues that factories are sited in the locations where costs (especially transport costs) are minimised and profits maximised. Accordingly, peripheral regions, for example, will normally be disadvantaged. But in small countries with highly developed transport networks the range of cost variation is generally so small as to render these ideas of little relevance except in a handful of industries in which transport costs are particularly significant.

The other unsatisfactory group of theories explains urban and regional growth in terms of cumulative causation. Unlike the spurious theories which suggest that regional problems will disappear automatically because of the operation of market forces, theories of cumulative causation maintain that areas will tend to diverge rather than converge in employment opportunities and living standards. The healthy growth of output in some areas, it is argued, leads to high investment and rapid increase in productivity, and hence greater competitiveness, which allows further increases in output and completes the virtuous circle. Leading regions are thus able to stay ahead of lagging regions which are unable to benefit from this spiral of rising output, investment and productivity. Theories of cumulative causation are particularly useful in explaining variations in growth between countries but their application to cities or regions is distinctly limited. The main problem at this smaller spatial scale is that the growth generated by factories in a successful city or region need not necessarily be retained within that area. In an economy dominated by large companies which each operate factories in many areas, growth generated in one part of the country is just as likely to be hived off into a new or existing factory elsewhere in the country, or even abroad. There is nothing arbitrary about this process. Often there may be good reasons why additions to output and employment should be directed to other areas, such as the lack of room for expansion in old urban factories, or the availability of capital grants in assisted areas. However, the effect is that the cumulative spiral in any one area is broken.

The most useful work on growth and decline has been largely non-theoretical, and has instead consisted of detailed empirical studies of what actually happened. This work includes attempts to measure the impact of the government's regional policy, studies of the movement of factories between areas and, more recently, investigation of the urban and regional pattern of company ownership and control. Considerable light has been shed on some aspects of employment change, but the main shortcoming of this research from a wider perspective is that it has been piecemeal. Several important influences have not been satisfactorily understood, and consequently it has not been possible to assess their relative importance or show how all the individual influences on growth add up to produce the overall pattern of change.

Our approach is also empirical but attempts to account for the pattern of unequal growth as a whole, rather than just one part of it. In this way we are able to establish which causes of growth and decline are important and which are simply trivial, and how the influences on employment change vary from place to place and from period to period. Also, where hard evidence was previously lacking we have painstakingly assembled new information rather than resort to unsubstantiated speculation or theory. Several popular explanations of urban and regional employment change are not supported by the facts; other less well-known explanations emerge as surprisingly important.

Understanding Growth and Decline

The popular picture of urban and regional growth in Britain, in which the South is growing and the North declining, dates from the inter-war years but continues to exert a powerful influence. Today it is at best only a partial description of the truth, as Chapter 2 demonstrates. For example London, at the heart of the South, has lost well over half a million manufacturing jobs during the last twenty years. To put this into perspective, London has lost almost as many manufacturing jobs as Scotland ever had. Indeed, some of the fastest-growing areas are found outside the traditionally prosperous South East and Midlands. The picture is, in fact, one of considerable complexity. As a general rule the differences within regions are far greater than the contrasts between them, the three main sectors— primary, manufacturing and services—sometimes show disparate trends at the regional or local scale, and the differences between individual industries can be as marked. Furthermore, during the last thirty years there have been some sharp changes in regional employment trends. Ironically, this complexity is our starting point in understanding urban and regional growth. A single all-embracing theory would have to be improbably sophisticated and subtle to explain the diversity which can be observed. A more plausible explanation is that there are several distinct causes of unequal growth, sometimes conflicting and sometimes working together in the same direction, which collectively produce the pattern of change.

In making sense out of the diversity the first helpful distinction is the traditional one between *basic* and *dependent* industries. Basic industries are those which sell their product outside the area, providing employment and bringing in income to the area from outside. Dependent industries are those which sell their product to the local market. In any city or region, the size of this local market is determined by the income brought into the area by basic industries, so that the growth of the dependent sector is ultimately determined by what happens to the basic sector. For example, employment in retailing, a dependent industry, cannot be expanded beyond what can be supported by the local market. Like all simple ideas the distinction between basic and dependent industries has its limitations, which will be discussed later, but on the whole these do little to reduce its usefulness. As is shown in Chapter 3, in the long run the location of employment change in the primary and manufacturing sectors, which are largely basic, is the main determinant of the location of employment change in the service sector, which is largely dependent. This is important because it means that the location of growth and decline in the primary and manufacturing sectors is the key to explaining the overall pattern of urban and regional employment change.

During the last twenty or thirty years the primary sector has had a major influence on the pattern of unequal growth. The main employers in this sector—agriculture and coalmining—have both shed jobs on a large scale during the post-war period, and those areas where they were substantial employers have suffered as a result. Indeed, looking back over the twentieth century as a whole, the huge loss of jobs in coalmining has been possibly the single most important cause of the persistently above average unemployment in much of Scotland, Wales and northern England. However, the primary sector need not concern us very much. As a result of the rapid decline in its employment, which caused so many problems in the past, the primary sector now employs so few people, except in one or two places, that it has ceased to exert a major influence on the overall pattern of growth and decline. Manufacturing, the other basic sector, therefore needs to be given most attention not simply because it is interesting in itself, but because the location of employment change in this sector is now the dominant influence on the pattern of urban and regional growth in Britain.

The de-industrialisation which the British economy is experiencing has led to lower levels of manufacturing employment in all areas, but de-industrialisation by itself does not explain why the growth and decline of this sector is so unevenly spread across the country. This book puts forward an explanation which is *structural*, by which we mean that manufacturing employment change in each area is dependent on the particular industrial characteristics inherited from the past. These characteristics are the product of many decades of investment and alter extremely slowly. Collectively, they exert a dominant influence on the urban and regional pattern of change in manufacturing industry.

The first structural characteristic is the mix of industries in each area, or *industrial structure* as it is generally known. In the country as a whole different industries experience different rates of employment change. This reflects a number of factors—changes in demand, the growth of labour productivity, and import penetration, for example—and results in unequal growth because the growing and declining industries are not evenly spread across all areas. An area dominated by nationally declining industries, for instance, will tend to experience large job losses. Although the idea that the mix of industries affects growth is an old one, the variable nature of this influence is not widely appreciated. Chapter 4 shows that though industrial structure was responsible for considerable divergences in growth up to the mid-1960s, it has subsequently become more-or-less irrelevant as an explanation of disparities in growth.

The second major structural factor, *urban structure*, has been the dominant influence on the pattern of employment change in recent years. Britain's cities are experiencing a rapid loss of manufacturing jobs while small towns and rural areas are quite successful in retaining and expanding their manufacturing base. As a general rule, the larger and more industrial a settlement the faster its decline. The loss of jobs from cities, and their inner areas in particular, is now well known, though it has been going on for much longer than most people realise, and Chapter 5 demonstrates the pervasiveness of the 'urban-rural shift'. The decline of manufacturing in cities and its growth in small towns is the main influence not only on the uneven growth within regions, but also on the differences between regions. The most urbanised regions, such as the North West, are experiencing the worst falls in industrial employment, while in regions characterised by small towns and rural areas, such as East Anglia, industry is more buoyant. Our evidence shows that the largest part of the urban-rural shift in employment reflects the failure of firms in cities to expand, compared to their rivals elsewhere, in the main, we believe, because the cramped sites and premises in urban areas do not meet the requirements of modern industry for increased floorspace.

The third structural element is the *size structure* of factories. This influences employment growth in an area because it is the main cause of variations in the rate of new-firm formation, described in Chapter 6. Despite their tiny initial size, new independent firms make an important contribution to employment change, partly through weight of numbers and partly because on average they experience healthy growth during their early years. A disproportionately large share of them are set up by people who have previously worked in small firms, so areas with a substantial heritage of existing small firms experience higher rates of new-firm formation than areas dominated by large factories. This has beneficial consequences for their long-term growth not only because new firms create employment, but also because these firms are small and thus maintain the existing favourable size structure.

The worst underlying trends in employment occur in areas with an adverse combination of these three structural characteristics. The

North West region, for example, has an unfavourable mix of industries (to a large extent because of its reliance on textiles) in a highly urban setting, and Merseyside, the one part of the region without declining textile and related industries, has one of the highest proportions of employment in very large factories. The consequence has been that the region has lost a quarter of its manufacturing jobs since the early 1950s, a much higher proportion than elsewhere in the country. In contrast, the virtuous combination of a neutral or favourable industrial structure, the lack of a conurbation, and a high proportion of employment in small firms, has pushed East Anglia, the South West and East Midland towards the top of the growth league.

Where structural disadvantages have caused job losses, the resulting problems have generally led to government intervention. *Regional policy*, described in Chapter 7, is the fourth major influence on the location of employment change, but one which differs from the others because it is a response to slow growth rather than an underlying cause of disparities. Regional policy has led to a shift of manufacturing jobs towards the assisted areas but its impact has diminished considerably in recent years. The role of government in favouring depressed regions at the expense of more prosperous areas is also evident in some of the trends in public service employment.

These four factors—industrial structure, urban structure, size structure and regional policy—are the focus of much of this book. These factors are given prominence not because a particular theory asserts that they must explain unequal growth, but because there is strong empirical evidence which demonstrates their role in determining the pattern of employment change. Their relative importance varies from place to place and from period to period but, as Chapter 8 argues, collectively they offer a satisfactory explanation for most of the urban and regional contrasts in manufacturing growth in post-war Britain.

The importance of structural factors emphasises the deeply ingrained nature of urban and regional problems. The mix of industries and the size of factories in any area are the outcome of a century or more of industrial development, and the urban structure has even older roots. Change in each case is inevitably slow, and though public policy might hope to accelerate the pace it cannot be expected to bring a swift transformation. It is therefore not surprising that though post-war regional policies have provided short-term benefit to the assisted areas, they have been much less successful in improving underlying trends and in creating the basis for self-sustaining growth. Rather than cause despair however, the depth of the problem should provide a better sense of what can be achieved within a given time-scale. Moreover, a proper understanding of how structural characteristics determine employment trends should enable the identification of those critical points where intervention can be most effective.

2 The Pattern of Change

One of the main reasons why urban and regional growth have been so poorly understood is that it has been exceptionally difficult to obtain a clear view of the changes which are occurring. Numerous revisions in definitions and methods of compilation mean that official statistics rarely allow a long view of growth and decline, a problem compounded by the complexity and instability of some employment trends. Consequently, some perceptions of the pattern of change, and the industrial location theories based upon them, have persisted long after they have ceased to offer an adequate description of employment trends in different parts of the country.

The starting point in explaining unequal growth must be an accurate description of employment change. The first part of this chapter therefore looks at changes in total employment, and the second at changes in the manufacturing sector. As we show later, manufacturing plays the crucial role in generating unequal growth, so it is worth singling out this sector to provide a more detailed description of change. In examining employment trends it is also useful to look at disparities within regions as well as between them, though at this stage, when our purpose is simply to describe what has happened, we will not show precisely how the two scales are linked. Our figures on employment change are based upon estimates produced by the Department of Employment. The methods we have used to derive figures which are comparable through time have been described fully elsewhere (Fothergill and Gudgin 1978), but an outline of this data is contained in Appendix A.

Changes in Total Employment

Total employment in the United Kingdom has fallen since 1966, when it reached an all-time peak, but by the end of the 1970s employment was still about ten per cent, or two million, higher than in the early 1950s. This modest growth over the last three decades has been unevenly spread between regions, as Table 2.1 and Figure 2.1 both demonstrate. At one extreme employment in East Anglia grew by over 40 per cent and showed no signs of any slackening after 1966, and the four fastest growing regions all achieved an increase in employment of at least double the national average. At the other

Table 2.1   *Regional employment change 1952–79*

	Per cent
East Anglia	+43.5
South West	+29.6
Northern Ireland	+22.4
East Midlands	+21.0
South East	+14.4
Wales	+10.0
North	+ 9.4
West Midlands	+ 8.3
Yorkshire & Humberside	+ 5.8
Scotland	+ 1.5
North West	− 5.2
U.K.	+10.6

extreme, by the end of the 1970s employment in the North West had fallen more than five per cent below even its 1952 level. Employment growth in Britain has therefore been not only disappointing, but unequal.

The most noticeable feature of the overall pattern of change is that it does not support the traditional 'north versus south' view of regional growth in Britain. The South East, which is normally thought of as Britain's leading growth zone, has in fact fared only marginally better than average, ranking fifth out of eleven regions, and the West Midlands, again a region often viewed as prosperous, has actually grown more slowly than the national average. Nevertheless, though the figures do not support the simple north versus south view of Britain, they do reveal one other major contrast: all the five slowest growing regions contain a conurbation, and the slowest growing region of all, the North West, contains two conurbations (Manchester and Merseyside). On the other hand, none of the four fastest growing regions contains a conurbation, and the fastest growing, East Anglia, is also the least urbanised. This strong urban-rural contrast in growth is a theme to which we will return.

Despite the academic and political concern which has been directed towards 'regions', they are not necessarily the most meaningful units with which to describe or explain the pattern of employment change. This is mainly because their basis in real life is distinctly limited. 'Regions' play little role in the life of their inhabitants. They are too small to be self-contained economies, but

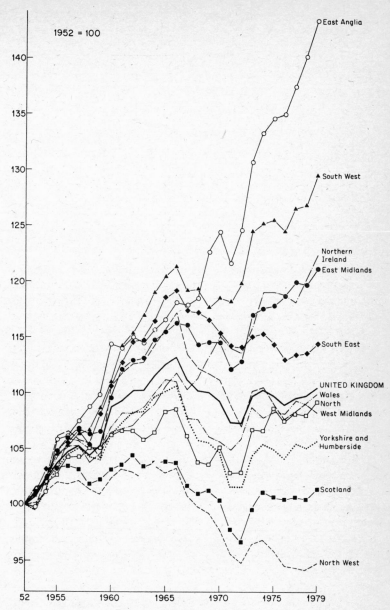

1952 = 100

Figure 2.1 Employment change by region 1952–79

too large to function as local labour markets, and particularly in England the regional level of government has never been properly developed. There is still a certain numerical convenience in aggregating data into large units such as regions, which no doubt explains the practice, but this should not blind us to the fact that these units obscure much more than they reveal. Nor should we necessarily assume that 'regional' contrasts must be explained by 'regional' factors. With these problems in mind, we therefore set about assembling information on differences in employment change within regions, as well as between them. For a rather shorter period, from 1959 to 1975, it is possible to examine employment change in each of sixty-one sub-regions in Great Britain. Once again it has been necessary to adjust the figures from the Department of Employment in order to provide a satisfactory comparison through time (see Appendix A).

A detailed description of the changes at the sub-regional scale has been presented elsewhere (Fothergill and Gudgin 1979a), but the overall picture which emerges from Figure 2.2 is one of complexity. The diversity within regions is considerable, confirming the suspicion that net change in any region is really only the sum of different and conflicting trends in each of the areas making up that region. For example, most of the South East has experienced rapid growth in total employment, though London has declined sharply, so that growth in the South East as a whole has been less impressive. The diversity of experience within Scotland, and within the Northern region, is even more marked. Nevertheless, despite this diversity at least one trend can be identified: all the sub-regions containing major conurbations—London, Birmingham, Manchester, Merseyside, Tyneside, West Yorkshire and Clydeside—have lost employment, while many rural areas, such as Cornwall, North Yorkshire and all of East Anglia, have experienced substantial growth. This suggests that hidden in the superficial pattern of diversity there may be more systematic 'urban-rural' differences.

In order to investigate possible urban-rural contrasts it is first necessary to group the sub-regions into broader categories which reflect their degree of urbanisation and industrialisation. This is difficult, and any classification is necessarily somewhat arbitrary because of the need to form discrete classes out of what is more nearly a continuum. The boundaries of the sub-regions themselves also pose a problem because some are drawn tightly around conurbations, for example, while others include large sections of hinterland. Bearing these problems in mind we have allocated each sub-region to one of six broad categories:

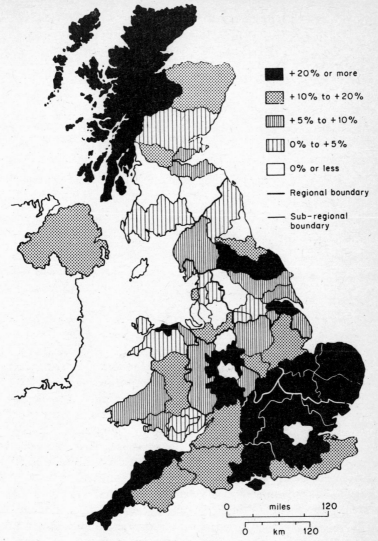

Figure 2.2 Employment change by sub-region 1959–75 (as percentage of 1959 employment)

1. *London*, which is unique in Britain in terms of its size.
2. *Conurbations.* The six largest industrial agglomerations, namely Manchester, Tyneside, Clydeside, Merseyside, Birmingham and West Yorkshire.

Table 2.2   Employment change by type of area 1959–75

	Per cent
London	−11.4
Conurbations	− 4.7
Free standing cities	+12.5
Industrial towns	+22.0
County towns	+18.0
Rural areas	+14.3
G.B.	+5.1

3. *Free standing cities.* Sub-regions dominated by medium-sized industrial cities, e.g. Sheffield and Coventry.
4. *Industrial towns.* Industrial areas made up mainly of smaller towns, e.g. North-East Lancashire and the Welsh valleys.
5. *County towns.* Traditionally rural areas containing at least one large town and a moderate amount of industry, e.g. Norfolk (including Norwich), plus coastal resorts, such as the Sussex coast.
6. *Rural areas.* Largely un-industrialised areas, e.g. rural Northumberland, Central Wales.

The allocation of sub-regions to each category is shown in Appendix B. Northern Ireland has been excluded because suitable sub-regional data is not available for this region.

Using this classification, it becomes immediately obvious that there are strong urban-rural contrasts in total employment change. Table 2.2 shows that as a general rule, the larger and more industrial a settlement the poorer its growth. The continuum is not perfect because the most rural areas have not fared as well as industrial or county towns, even though they have grown considerably faster than the national average. Moreover, not every individual sub-region shows a rate of growth which is close to the average for its type. In each sub-region there are factors which affect growth over and above those which characterise each type of area, and later we devote a great deal of attention to explaining contrasts within each category as well as between them. The important point to note here, however, is that when sub-regions are grouped into broad categories these other variations in growth disappear and more systematic urban-rural contrasts show up.

The Manufacturing Sector
Just as employment change in any region is no more than the sum of changes in its components parts, so changes in total employment are

Table 2.3   *Manufacturing employment change by region 1952–79*

	Per cent
East Anglia	+70.3
South West	+25.7
Wales	+17.5
East Midlands	+11.4
North	+ 7.8
West Midlands	− 7.8
South East	− 9.9
Yorkshire & Humberside	−13.7
Scotland	−18.4
North West	−24.5
Northern Ireland	−27.4
U.K.	− 7.8

really only the sum of changes in several distinct industries. Among these, manufacturing plays a crucial role in generating unequal growth, so it is appropriate to complement the description of changes in total employment with a brief description of changes in this sector.

The large regional differences in manufacturing employment change are demonstrated by Table 2.3, for the period from 1952 to 1979. The ordering of the regions differs in detail from Table 2.1 (for total employment), but again the unevenness of growth is very marked. Indeed, the contrasts in manufacturing employment change have been almost twice as large as those for total employment and the gap between the two extremes, East Anglia (+ 70.3 per cent) and Northern Ireland (− 27.4 per cent), can only be described as dramatic. Once more too, the pattern of change does not conform to a simple 'north versus south' stereotype: though two southern regions, East Anglia and the South West have shown the best growth, the South East has actually fared worse than average. The numbers of jobs associated with this uneven growth have been very large indeed. For example, the East Midlands, which ranks only fourth among the high-flyers, expanded its manufacturing employment by nearly 20 per cent, or 100,000 jobs, relative to the U.K. as a whole, while the relative decline of the North West has meant that by 1979 it had over 230,000 manufacturing jobs fewer than if it had grown at the national rate.

An important aspect of the growth of regional manufacturing employment is that it has also varied through time. The unevenness arises from three separate sources. Firstly, manufacturing employ-

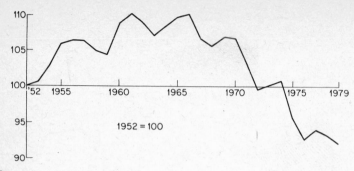

Figure 2.3   U.K. manufacturing employment 1952–79

ment in the British economy has fluctuated with the trade cycle, shown in Figure 2.3, and this cyclical pattern can be observed in every region. During the severe recession that occurred between 1974 and 1976, for example, when U.K. manufacturing employment fell by eight per cent, manufacturing employment fell substantially in all regions, including prosperous regions such as East Anglia. Secondly, U.K. manufacturing employment experienced a sharp change in trend during the post-war period. Until the mid-1960s it increased, as output rose faster than labour productivity, reaching a peak in 1966 at just over ten per cent above its level in the early 1950s. Thereafter manufacturing employment has fallen sharply. Between 1966 and 1973 labour productivity surged forward, outstripping the growth in output, so that employment fell. Since 1973 the growth of productivity has slowed but the decline in output has ensured that manufacturing employment continues to fall at an alarming rate. The consequence has been that every region has experienced slower growth (or faster decline) in manufacturing employment since 1966, and only the two fastest-growing regions— East Anglia and the South West—were able to achieve any increase at all between 1966 and 1979.

If the national decline in manufacturing employment in recent years had reflected vigorous investment in new technology and production processes, leading to rising labour productivity and greater resilience against foreign competition at home and abroad, the loss of manufacturing jobs might not have been entirely unwelcome. A viable and internationally competitive manufacturing sector would have generated wealth which could have supported a much greater expansion of service employment—particularly in the public services—and levels of unemployment would thus have been kept down. In the event, of course, declining employment in British

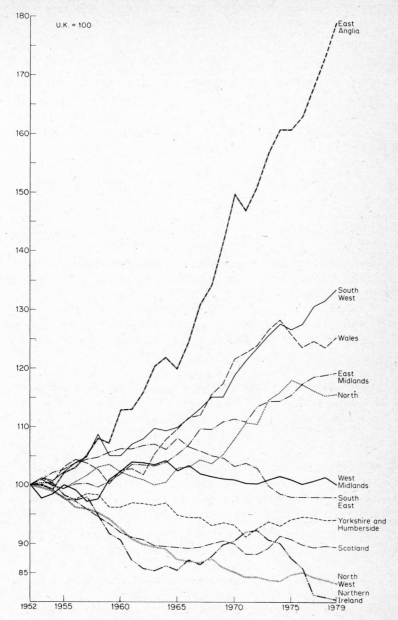

Figure 2.4   Manufacturing employment change relative to the U.K. 1952–79

manufacturing has reflected its weakness, not its strength. Indeed, there can be little doubt that if the performance of manufacturing had not been so weak, overall employment would now be higher and unemployment lower in *all* regions. Insofar as some regions, such as the South East, are now experiencing substantial unemployment for the first time, or insofar as employment losses in other regions, such as Scotland, have accelerated, much of the blame must be placed on the declining competitiveness and employment of British manufacturing industry as a whole.

The third cause of the fluctuations in the growth of manufacturing employment in each region is that regional trends have not always been consistent, as Figure 2.4 shows. Several regions—East Anglia, the North West, South West and East Midlands—have experienced manufacturing employment growth which has been consistently better or worse than the U.K. as a whole. This in itself is quite remarkable, given the length of the period (nearly 30 years), and testifies to the strength and stability of some of the underlying causes of regional growth differences. Other regions show a change in trend relative to the U.K. as a whole. From the early 1960s onwards there was a marked improvement in Wales and the North in particular, and a deterioration in the South East and, to a lesser extent, in the West Midlands. These changes in trend are not in any way random and, as will be seen later, at least part of the change in the early 1960s can be attributed to regional policy.

During the second half of the 1970s manufacturing employment trends in these regions altered once more: the relative growth of the North and Wales appears to have come to an end, and the relative decline of the South East has eased too. Northern Ireland is worth singling out for special comment. The region's relative improvement in the 1960s turned into a dramatic collapse in the 1970s, which placed it firmly at the bottom of the manufacturing growth league. The change of trend in this region was much sharper than elsewhere and must surely reflect Northern Ireland's unique political circumstances. Of all the influences on regional manufacturing growth, none is apparently as harmful as widespread political violence.

Though the regional pattern of manufacturing employment change has been uneven, the enormity of some of the disparities becomes apparent only at the sub-regional scale, shown in Figure 2.5. During the shorter period between 1959 and 1975 (the regional figures were for 1952 to 1979) 11 sub-regions grew by more than 50 per cent, while 9 sub-regions lost more than 10 per cent of their manufacturing employment. At the two extremes, London lost nearly four out of every ten of its manufacturing jobs during these sixteen years, while

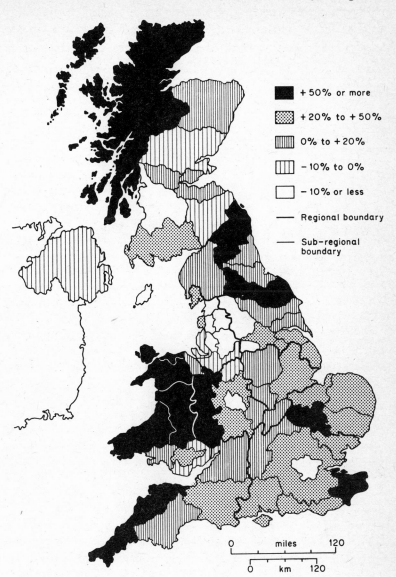

+ 50% or more

+ 20% to + 50%

0% to + 20%

− 10% to 0%

− 10% or less

Regional boundary

Sub-regional boundary

Figure 2.5 Manufacturing employment change by sub-region 1959–75 (as percentage of 1959 manufacturing employment)

in Central Wales manufacturing employment quadrupled. Disparities such as these are much larger than those in the growth of total employment in each sub-region.

Table 2.4   *Manufacturing employment change by type of area 1959–75*

	Per cent
London	−37.8
Conurbations	−15.9
Free standing cities	+ 4.8
Industrial towns	+16.3
County towns	+28.8
Rural areas	+77.2
G.B.	− 5.2

As with total employment, there is little in the pattern of manufacturing employment change which is 'regional'. Within regions there is often considerable diversity, which again suggests that regions are really no more than the sum of their disparate parts, rather than meaningful economic entities. But the sub-regional diversity is far from random because, when the sub-regions are grouped together into our six types of area (Table 2.4) a striking picture emerges. Large urban sub-regions have done badly; rural sub-regions have grown very quickly. The contrast is large and remarkably consistent. Once again, not every sub-region has grown at the average rate for its type, but a closer look reveals that almost without exception the county towns and rural areas have grown faster than any of the conurbations or free standing cities.

Of course there is nothing new in the finding that manufacturing employment is declining in London and the conurbations. Since the mid-1970s politicians and civil servants have been acutely aware of this problem, and in particular the decline of the inner city. The press, too, have given a great deal of coverage to the deprivation and decline in Britain's big cities. Our figures show that as far as manufacturing is concerned, the picture is not simply one of decline in the cities and growth elsewhere. In fact there is a clear relationship between the size of the settlements in a sub-region and its manufacturing growth: small cities grow faster than large cities, just as small towns grow faster than large towns.

One could be forgiven for believing that the decline of the cities is a comparatively recent phenomenon, in view of the surge of publicity on this subject in recent years, but Table 2.5 shows that manufacturing has been undergoing a marked shift out of the cities towards more rural locations since at least the end of the 1950s. Certainly, in more recent years the *absolute* loss of manufacturing

Table 2.5   *Manufacturing employment change by type of area and period 1959–75*

	as % per year of manufacturing employment at the start of each period		
	1959–66	1966–71	1971–5
London	−0.7	−3.6	−3.1
Conurbations	+0.2	−1.7	−3.2
Free standing cities	+1.7	−0.1	−2.3
Industrial towns	+2.8	−0.2	−1.5
County towns	+3.0	+1.1	+0.1
Rural areas	+6.0	+1.9	+3.5
G.B.	+1.1	−1.1	−1.8

jobs in London and the conurbations has accelerated, but this has been a manifestation of the declining fortunes of British manufacturing as a whole. The *relative* loss of jobs compared to the national average, and compared to smaller towns and rural areas, has been consistently high during each of the three periods shown in Table 2.5. Looking even further back in time, however, it seems that the urban-rural shift did accelerate quite sharply around 1960. Moore, Rhodes and Tyler have compiled data on employment trends by type of area as far back as 1951. Table 2.6, which presents their figures, shows that the gap between London and the conurbations on the one hand, and 'hinterland' areas on the other, was much smaller in the 1950s than subsequently, though even in this early

Table 2.6   *Manufacturing employment change by type of area 1951–61 and 1961–76*

	as % per year of 1951 manufacturing employment	
	1951–61	1961–76
London	−0.1	−3.0
Conurbations[1]	−0.2	−1.5
Free standing cities[1]	−0.2	−1.1
Hinterlands	+1.3	+1.4
G.B.	+0.5	−0.5

[1]Definitions are not comparable with our own classification of areas. See Appendix B.
Source: Moore, Rhodes and Tyler (1980).

period a shift of manufacturing jobs out of the cities was occurring.

It is perhaps surprising that the decline of the cities has taken so long to become widely recognised as a problem, given that it has been going on for some considerable time. The explanation probably has a great deal to do with the changing fortunes of the British economy as a whole. For many years the exodus from large cities was actively promoted, through the New Towns programme for example, in the belief that overcrowding was a worse evil, and this decentralisation of industry could be achieved relatively painlessly when unemployment was low nearly everywhere. Since the early 1970s, however, the decline of manufacturing in the cities has led to unemployment because fewer alternative jobs have been available. What was previously regarded as a desirable trend therefore became regarded as a problem.

Alternatively, the fact that the decline of the cities has only recently attracted so much attention could be attributed to the sluggishness of geographers, economists and planners in identifying what is going on. Many researchers are only now beginning to recognise that the shift from urban to rural areas is the major trend in industrial location in Britain, even though the shift has been taking place for at least twenty years. It is a tribute to the strength of prevailing ideologies and perceptions—in particular to the 'north versus south' view of Britain—that the urban-rural shift has taken so long to gain the prominence it deserves.

3 The Leading Role of Manufacturing

Because an industrial economy is made up of many highly interconnected sectors with large flows of goods, services and payments between them, it is not easy to see where economic growth originates. In the world as a whole, growth occurs simultaneously in several or even all sectors. It derives from the expansion of inputs—labour, cultivated land, raw materials, energy and capital equipment—and from improvements in the efficiency of using each of these things. But though growth occurs in many component parts of the industrial economy, those parts are not necessarily of equal importance in *causing* economic growth. In fact, what happens is that the growth and development of some sectors generates the wealth and income which in turn can support an expansion in other sectors. This is a particularly important distinction in a small area, such as a city or a region, because a small area normally lacks the capacity to meet all its needs from within its own boundaries, and must therefore trade with the rest of the world. The heavy reliance on trade means that the expansion of those sectors which sell their products to outside the area is crucial in providing income both to finance essential imports and to be spent on locally produced goods and services.

The sectors which play this leading role in urban and regional growth need to be identified in order to understand what causes unequal growth. This chapter goes about this task in two stages: firstly, by quantifying the importance of each major sector in employment change, and secondly by examining the interdependency between changes in those sectors. Despite the size and growth of service employment, the conclusion which emerges is that manufacturing has become the dominant influence on the pattern of urban and regional employment change in Britain. This conclusion enables later chapters to focus attention on manufacturing and the causes of its uneven growth.

National Change in Each Sector

For descriptive purposes we have divided the economy into five sectors—agriculture, mining, manufacturing, construction and

Table 3.1   U.K. employment change by sector 1952–79

	Employment in 1952	Change 1952–79	
	thousands	thousands	% 1952 *total* employment
Agriculture	740	− 441	− 2.1
Mining	885	− 541	− 2.6
Manufacturing	8,285	− 646	− 3.1
Construction & utilities	1,755	− 68	− 0.3
Services	9,172	+3,901	+18.7
Total	20,837	+2,205	+10.6

utilities, and services. This division has its roots in the nature of the activities they each perform, but in the British context these broad categories are doubly relevant because of the contrasting changes in employment which the five sectors have experienced. Table 3.1 shows that between 1952 and 1979 agriculture and mining both shed over half their employment, equal to a decline of nearly one million jobs in total. The decline has slowed in recent years but has been unbroken throughout the post-war period. In agriculture, job losses have been due to a rapid rise in productivity brought about by mechanisation, while in mining the decline in output, as oil and natural gas displaced coal as a source of power, has been as important as increases in productivity. Manufacturing also shed nearly 650,000 jobs, though because of its much larger absolute size as an employer this represents a smaller proportional decline than in agriculture or mining. Unlike agriculture and mining, manufacturing employment trends changed dramatically in the mid-1960s. Between 1952 and 1966 manufacturing employment rose by around 850,000; thereafter, up to 1979, it declined by 1.5 million, followed by a further dramatic decline in 1980. Employment in construction and utilities (gas, water and electricity) fell very slightly over the full period, though again this hides an increase up to the mid-1960s and a decline thereafter.

However, the striking feature of Table 3.1 is the large expansion of service employment—nearly four million jobs—which was more than sufficient to offset the losses in the other sectors and provided a net increase in total employment of a little more than ten per cent over the whole period. The growth of the service sector has been remarkable and has persisted even during the austere economic climate of recent years. Throughout the post-war period, but especially in recent years, its share of total employment has grown steadily. By the end of the 1970s nearly six out of every ten employees were engaged in service activities, and on the basis of current trends the day cannot be too far off when services will employ twice as many people as the entire manufacturing sector. Britain is not alone in this respect, because every other advanced industrial economy is also experiencing growth in its service sector. In the United States, which is often looked upon as an indication of things to come, the share of total employment in services is higher than in Britain, and still rising.

Not surprisingly, a view which is gaining popularity is that the growth of service employment will offset the erosion of Britain's manufacturing base. The decline in manufacturing may not exactly be welcome, but it does at least allow the economy to specialise in those sorts of activities which the British are supposedly 'good at', such as insurance, banking and finance. Some proponents of this view go as far as to argue that the prosperous economy of the future will displace manufacturing by office activities, just as at an earlier stage of development manufacturing displaced agriculture. To subsidise ailing manufacturing industries and to obstruct the growth of services is therefore 'to deny the logic of the free market and to stand in the way of progress and the evolution of the "post-industrial society"'. Although this faith in the service sector is misplaced, it cannot be denied that there has been a remarkable redirection of employment away from industry and into services, and this trend has been sufficiently powerful to have had a major impact on employment in all parts of the country. Before we go any further therefore, it is important to look at why this has happened.

The Growth of Service Employment

The main cause of the service sector's increasing share of total employment is its slow growth of labour productivity. Table 3.2 shows that between 1952 and 1979 the increase in service sector output was roughly comparable to the increase in manufacturing output. Yet while labour productivity increased by 115 per cent in manufacturing—rather faster than the growth of output—productivity in services increased by only 29 per cent, or about one per cent a year. Consequently, as employment in manufacturing fell, service employment expanded by over 40 per cent in order to produce the additional output.

These figures must be treated a little cautiously because there are difficulties in measuring service sector output: unlike manufactur-

Table 3.2   Output, productivity and employment by sector 1979

| | 1952 = 100 | | |
	Output[1]	Productivity[2]	Employment
Agriculture	173	433	40
Mining[3]	61	149	41
Manufacturing	198	215	92
Construction and utilities	196	204	96
Services	185	129	143

[1] at constant prices.
[2] output per employee.
[3] 1975
Source: output from National Income and Expenditure blue books.

ing, in much of the service sector there is no finite output which can be easily quantified and monitored from year to year. However, it is not difficult to understand why productivity should rise so slowly in the service sector. In education, health and personal services, there is little or no scope for achieving increases in labour productivity through mechanisation, and even in office activities labour-saving technology, such as the computer, is a comparatively recent and far from universal innovation. Improvements in the quality of some services actually necessitates an *increase* in the labour input. The reduction of pupil-teacher ratios, which has been pursued as a matter of policy, is a good example.

Because productivity grows more slowly in services, an increase in their share of total employment is inevitable if the production of services is allowed to keep up with the production of commodities, which no doubt explains why the same trend is found in other countries as well as Britain. To a large extent too, an increase in the share of public sector services is inevitable for the same reasons. A large proportion of public services—teaching and social services for example—offer no scope for raising productivity through mechanisation, so the employment in these activities must increase if public services are to be improved as living standards rise. These are simple but crucial points which are often overlooked.

However, at least some of the expansion of service jobs is misleading. Department of Employment figures show that between 1971 and 1976 service employment rose by 1.2 million, but the increase in part-time employment among women accounted for no less than two-thirds of the growth—800,000 jobs—and the increase in part-time male employment for a further 100,000. The growth in the input of labour to the service sector has therefore been considerably smaller than superficial figures suggest. Moreover, because part-time female employment tends to be poorly paid, and because on average the service sector pays lower wages than manufacturing, the impact on levels of household income has probably been less than the large expansion in employment would give one to believe. The composition of the increase in the workforce in services also debunks the myth that the growing service sector, and in particular the public sector, has 'poached' labour from manufacturing and thus hastened its decline. Given that the fall in manufacturing employment has been mainly among full-time men while the expansion in services has been mainly among part-time women, it is hard to see how the service sector has crowded out manufacturing in any scramble for labour.

Probably the best guide to the role of services in economic growth is their contribution to the balance of payments, which is particularly important in Britain. As a small country which cannot provide enough food for its population nor supply all its raw materials, Britain must rely on what it can sell abroad in order to pay for imports and sustain its standard of living. The fact that in recent years there has also been a sharp rise in the volume of imported manufactures makes exporting doubly important. The contribution of the service sector to export earnings should therefore be a good indicator of its contribution to the growth of the economy as a whole.

Service exports include earnings from a diverse range of activities, such as tourism, insurance and banking, shipping and aircraft, and professional business services, but in 1978 they totalled less than half the value of exports from the manufacturing sector, only £12,000 million, compared to £26,000 million from manufacturing. Exports per employee in services were only a quarter of those in manufacturing. Moreover, between 1966 and 1978 there was no tendency for the volume of service exports to rise any faster than the volume of manufactured exports. At the national scale, therefore, the evidence does not support the view than the service sector is leading economic growth. It is certainly true that this sector's share of total employment has risen, but this is really a consequence rather than a cause of economic growth.

The Contribution of Each Sector to Urban and Regional Growth

National trends in employment in each sector have an important impact on employment in all areas. Tables 3.3 and 3.4, which deal

Table 3.3 Employment change by sector and region 1952–79

| | | | | Construction | | |
	Agriculture	Mining	Manufacturing	& utilities	Services	Total
				as % *total* employment in each region in *1952*		
East Anglia	−12.6	+ 0.4	+19.1	+1.6	+35.0	+43.5
South West	− 4.0	− 0.5	+ 7.8	−0.6	+27.1	+29.6
Northern Ireland	− 1.8	− 0.3	−12.1	+2.7	+34.0	+22.4
East Midlands	− 3.1	− 4.4	+ 5.0	+0.8	+22.7	+21.0
South East	− 1.6	− 0.1	+ 3.4	−2.0	+21.4	+14.4
Wales	− 2.3	−11.5	+ 5.3	+1.3	+17.3	+10.0
North	− 1.9	−11.1	+ 2.7	+2.2	+17.6	+ 9.4
West Midlands	− 1.6	− 2.1	− 4.3	+0.4	+16.0	+ 8.3
Yorkshire & Humberside	− 1.5	− 3.9	− 6.3	+0.6	+16.9	+ 5.8
Scotland	− 2.8	− 3.4	− 6.8	+0.8	+13.7	+ 1.5
North West	− 0.8	− 1.7	−11.9	−1.2	+10.4	− 5.2
U.K.	− 2.1	− 2.6	− 3.1	−0.3	+18.7	+10.6

Table 3·4 Employment change by sector and type of area 1959–75

	Agriculture	Mining	Manufacturing	Services[1]	Total
				as % *total* employment in each area in 1952	
London	−0.3	0	−13.0	+ 1.9	−11.4
Conurbations	−0.3	−2.4	− 7.9	+ 5.9	− 4.7
Free standing cities	−1.0	−3.6	+ 1.1	+16.0	+12.5
Industrial towns	−1.4	−4.6	+ 6.9	+21.1	+22.0
County towns	−4.6	−0.1	+ 7.5	+15.2	+18.0
Rural areas	−6.5	−1.7	+11.1	+11.4	+14.3
G.B.	−1.3	−2.2	− 2.2	+10.8	+ 5.1

[1]includes construction and utilities.

with regions and types of area respectively, show the contribution which each sector has made to total employment change in different parts of the country. In these tables the change in each sector is expressed as a percentage of *total* employment in each area at the start of the period, so that we can see its relative importance in overall employment change.

In line with national trends, services have provided an increase in employment everywhere. Even in the slowest growing region, the North West, service growth has been sufficient to add ten per cent to total employment. Similarly, in almost all areas agriculture and mining have declined. The contribution of manufacturing has been more variable, which is not surprising because we have already noted the large differences in the rate at which this sector has grown up and down the country. In some areas manufacturing has been responsible for a sizable increase in total employment, and in others a sizable loss.

The contrasting experience of different regions is interesting. Despite massive job losses in agriculture in East Anglia, a larger growth in manufacturing kept this region at the top of the league, whereas the North West, which lost hardly any jobs in agriculture, still ended up at the bottom. Similar levels of total employment change also hide disparities between individual sectors. For example, though the growth in total employment was much the same in Northern Ireland and the East Midlands, manufacturing provided a much larger increase in the East Midlands, and services in Northern Ireland. A more general point which also emerges is that many of the areas which experienced substantial job losses in agriculture and mining also experienced above average growth in manufacturing, so the resulting changes in total employment have been more modest than they might otherwise have been.

The contribution which each sector makes to employment change in any area depends on the initial importance of that sector as much as on its rate of growth. The rural areas illustrate this point. The previous chapter showed that their manufacturing employment grew by no less than 77 per cent between 1959 and 1975 (Table 2.4), even though national manufacturing employment declined slightly between these years. However, at the start of this period the proportion of employment in rural areas in manufacturing was particularly low—only 14 per cent of all jobs, compared to 40 per cent nationally. Therefore, despite the impressive rate of growth in manufacturing employment in rural areas, the increase in their *total* employment attributable to manufacturing was much more modest—only 11 per cent (Table 3.4). Indeed, at the end of the 1950s agriculture was still as large an employer as manufacturing in rural areas, which meant that subsequent changes in agricultural employment were particularly important to these areas. Britain's rural areas are an extreme case, at least so far as the relative importance of agriculture and manufacturing is concerned, but the balance between major sectors does vary sufficiently up and down the country to have a substantial impact on employment change.

Historically, agriculture has been important in East Anglia, where it still employed as many as one in five of all workers in the early 1950s, so it is not surprising to find that agriculture has been a major source of job loss in this region. Mining (mostly coalmining) has traditionally accounted for a large share of total employment in Wales and the North, and to a lesser extent in the East Midlands and Yorkshire and Humberside, but has been negligible in several other areas. Again, where mining has been a major employer it has also been responsible for a large decline in total employment. Manufacturing and services tend to be spread more evenly, though the ratio between the two does still vary from place to place. As a general rule the percentage of the workforce in manufacturing tends to be low where the primary sector is important. The proportion in service activities is high in London and the South East, the South West, in county towns and rural areas, but below average in the Midland regions.

During the post-war period some of the sharpest contrasts in the balance between sectors have disappeared, mainly because of the diminished importance of agriculture and mining, though this should not be allowed to obscure the sizable influence which such differences have had on the pattern of employment change in recent decades. A high proportion of employment in agriculture or mining, for example, has proved a severe handicap to overall employment growth in some regions, such as East Anglia and Wales. Insofar as some of the disparities in the balance between sectors persist, they continue to play an important role in determining employment change in different areas. In particular, the balance between manufacturing and service employment seems likely to play an increasing role as the brunt of the decline in the British economy is borne by the manufacturing sector. A region such as the West Midlands, where 45 per cent of all employees are in manufacturing, is clearly more at risk than the South East, where the proportion is now only 25 per cent.

Basic and Dependent Industries

So far we have looked only at the statistical importance of each sector's contribution to overall employment change. However, if two sectors each account for an increase in total employment of say ten per cent, this does not mean that they are therefore of equal importance in *causing* growth. An increase of ten per cent in one sector may in fact lead directly to part, or the whole, of the increase in the other. The important distinction is the one already made in our introduction, between those sectors which are *basic* and those which are *dependent*. Basic industries, we recall, are those which sell their product outside the area, thus bringing in income from outside; dependent industries are those which sell their product to the local market—either to consumers, or to the basic industries themselves. Because the size of the local market depends on the income brought in by basic industries, the growth of the dependent sector will be determined by what happens to the basic sector.

Of course, this is an oversimplification. In practice income is brought into an area by other routes, as well as by basic industries. For example, central government spending on pensions and social security benefits brings money into an area, which in turn supports jobs in dependent industries, such as retailing and public transport. In addition certain industries which serve the local population, such as health and education, are supported directly by public expenditure—mostly financed by central government—rather than by local consumer spending. And dependent industries themselves provide their employees with the income which will support still more dependent jobs.

None of these points invalidates the basic-dependent split. What they do mean is that in the short and medium term, perhaps a decade or even more, the link between changes in the basic sector and changes in the dependent sector can be tenuous. If a steelworks closes, for example, this is likely to be followed fairly quickly by a second-round loss of jobs in those local firms which relied on the steelworks for business, such as haulage contractors. The reduction in earnings from employment will be partly offset by unemployment benefits and by redundancy payments, so local consumer spending and the jobs which depend on it, in shops and public houses for example, will not fall so dramatically.

Even if some of the businesses dependent on the local market do feel the pinch, it may be some time before this begins to affect their employment, and the closure of the steelworks will of course make no immediate difference to local schools and hospitals. Children still have to go to school, whether or not their fathers are in work. The second-round loss of jobs may therefore not be very large at first. In the long run however, if the closure of the steelworks is not offset by the growth of a new basic industry, the size of the local dependent sector will begin to fall. Some people will move elsewhere in search of work. When they move, the demand for local consumer services will fall again, as will the demand for school places and hospital beds. Employment in the dependent sector will thus eventually be reduced to a level which can be supported by the new lower level of basic employment in the area.

Deciding exactly which industries are basic and which are dependent is a thorny problem. This is partly because the split will vary a little from place to place: a larger region, for example, will normally be able to supply more of its needs for industrial inputs or for specialised services from within its own boundaries. Partly, the problem is that some industries contain both basic and dependent elements. For the moment, however, we are concerned only to establish which of the five sectors into which we have divided the economy are mainly basic in any city or region, and which are mainly dependent.

Agriculture and mining must be classed as mainly basic. Their location depends on the availability of natural resources—farmland and minerals—rather than on local markets. The fact that agriculture is a major employer in East Anglia, but unimportant in the North West for example, has nothing to do with the size of the local market for agricultural produce in these two regions. In contrast, construction and utilities (gas, water and electricity) are dependent industries. Their employment in any area depends mainly, though not entirely, on the demand from local consumers and firms. This is reflected in the relatively uniform proportion of total employment which is engaged in construction and utilities in each region.

Manufacturing is more difficult because within this sector there are some industries which are basic and others which are dependent. Baking and brewing are two examples of manufacturing industries which serve primarily local markets and which must be classed as dependent. But these industries are unusual because at the regional scale, let alone in small local areas, Britain's manufacturing economy is very 'open', selling a high proportion of its output abroad or to other regions—an impression confirmed by the available evidence, such as a recent study of the structure of the Scottish economy (Fraser of Allander Institute 1978). In the context of British cities and regions, the conclusion must be that manufacturing industry is mainly basic. Such a simplistic categorisation overstates the case a little, but in Chapter 4 we look more closely at the precise balance between basic and dependent activities in manufacturing.

Services: A Dependent Sector?

The service sector is difficult to classify. The main problem is its sheer diversity and the complexity of the different channels through which service activities are supported in any particular location. Arguably, all those service jobs which are not supported by the expenditure of income which is earned locally should be defined as basic, including those jobs in public services which are financed by central government. However, this definition of basic services is inappropriate because the level of provision of public services in any area is strongly tied to population levels, and so too are a great many government transfer payments, such as pensions and social security.

As we have argued, in the long run a loss of basic jobs can be expected to lead to out-migration, and thus to a reduction in population, in which case population-related services ought properly to be classed as dependent industries. 'Basic services' are therefore more appropriately defined as those service activities which are not tied to local populations or markets. The sorts of activities which might be described as basic to any city or region include head offices, specialised business services (such as those in the City of London), ports, airports and universities. Their growth is not affected by what happens to employment in the rest of the local economy in which they are located, so they function very much as an independent motor of growth and decline.

There are still problems in determining which service activities are basic, because the larger the area concerned the smaller the proportion that will be basic. For example, most large towns perform an important function as service centres for their hinterlands, providing a range of administrative, retailing and professional services which are not found in surrounding areas. If these towns are considered in isolation from their hinterlands much of their service sector must be described as basic, in that it is supported by demand from outside the towns themselves, but taking the towns and hinterlands together, the same service functions are clearly not basic.

At the regional scale the share of service employment which is basic is probably not large, and to illustrate this point Table 3.5 groups the main service industries which might be considered to be basic and compares their employment with that in dependent services. The definition of basic services which we have used is generous, including external transport services (railways, air, ports,

Table 3.5   Industrial distribution of U.K. service employment

	Per cent	
	1959	1977
Railways, ports, road haulage, sea and air transport	9.7	6.4
Insurance, banking, finance and business services (50%)	3.0	4.4
Other professional services (inc. R and D)	3.0	3.7
Hotels	2.2	2.1
National government (50%)	2.6	2.5
Basic services	20.5	19.1
Post and telecommunications	3.1	3.3
Retailing and wholesaling	26.3	21.3
Health and education	15.4	24.4
Local government	7.3	7.4
Garages	3.3	3.5
Entertainment (pubs, betting, sport, cinema etc.)	6.3	6.9
Rest of insurance etc. and national government	5.6	6.9
Other services	12.2	7.2
Dependent services	79.5	80.9
All services	100.0	100.0

Source: Department of Employment.

shipping and road haulage), hotels, research and development, and half of the employment in each of insurance, banking, finance, business services and national government. Still, the conclusion is striking. Even on these generous assumptions only about one in five of all service jobs might be considered basic. Employment in education and health—two services overwhelmingly tied to local population—together now exceeds the employment in all basic services by a sizable margin. Furthermore, there is no evidence that the share of basic services is rising through time. The conclusion must be that the service sector is mainly 'dependent'.

In recent years insurance, banking and business services have been regarded as a bright spot in Britain's economy, and it has not escaped the notice of politicians that because this industry is growing, and because some parts of it are potentially foot-loose, it might play an important role in regional policy. The extension of some forms of regional assistance to the service sector reflects these sentiments. Unfortunately the service sector as a whole is too often viewed as being composed largely of these sorts of business services, with the result that too much faith is placed in its potential for regional policy. What is overlooked, and what is demonstrated by

Table 3.5, is that a more accurate description of the service sector would be that it is dominated by activities such as health, education and retailing, which are tied to local population and markets. Basic services, including business services, are really only a small part of service employment. Moreover, as even a great deal of the employment in basic services is not locationally mobile—it is hard to imagine very many of the functions of the City of London willingly decentralising to the regions, for example—the potential for a successful regional policy in the service sector must be very restricted indeed.

Some indication of the location of basic service jobs can be obtained from Table 3.6, which shows the share of total employment held by services in each region. Employment in many dependent services such as education and retailing is a fairly constant proportion of total employment in each region, so the share of employment in dependent services as a whole is unlikely to vary much between regions. Consequently, where the percentage in services is particularly high this presumably indicates the presence of basic services, or where it is low their absence. Northern Ireland is an exception to this rule because the high proportion in services in this region reflects an unusually rapid expansion in public services in recent years.

The lowest proportion of employment in services is found in the East and West Midlands, where it is likely that the service jobs are almost entirely in dependent activities. Partly as a result of their relative proximity to London, both regions lack business and financial services beyond the minimum necessary to serve local

Table 3.6   Share of services in total employment by region 1979

	Per cent
South East	66
Northern Ireland	62
South West	60
Scotland	57
U.K.	*57*
East Anglia	54
North West	54
Wales	54
North	53
Yorkshire and Humberside	50
East Midlands	46
West Midlands	44

Source: Department of Employment.

industry. Tourism is not well developed in either region, both lack major ports and port-related services, and both regions contain few major offices of central government. Roughly 45 per cent of total employment in the East and West Midlands is in services, compared to 57 per cent in the country as a whole. Assuming that the proportion in dependent services in other regions is similar to the Midlands figure, then the difference between the Midlands and national figures—12 per cent or a little more than one in five of all service jobs—probably represents basic service employment. This supports our earlier estimate that only about one in five service jobs in the country as a whole are basic to the region in which they are located.

The Role of Services in Regional Growth

If the simple division into basic and dependent sectors is at all meaningful it should be possible to identify a strong relationship between the two. Figure 3.1 compares employment change in the basic sectors (agriculture, mining and manufacturing) with change in the dependent service sector (including construction and utilities) for each region between 1952 and 1979, and shows that excepting the anomaly of Northern Ireland, employment changes in the two are closely related. Over the period as a whole there was a substantial growth in service employment relative to basic sector employment. A region in which there was no net change in basic employment could still expect its total employment to grow by more than a quarter solely as a result of the expansion of service employment.

Variations in service growth, however, have depended closely on change in other sectors. Very roughly, for every one percentage point change in total employment arising in the basic sectors, there has been an additional one percentage point change arising in the service sector. This is equivalent to a long-term 'economic base multiplier' of 2.0. Brown (1972) conducted some similar analyses for 1921–61 and for 1951–61 and concluded that the long-term economic base multiplier was 1.7—or, in other words, that 10 more basic sector jobs create 7 more service jobs. The difference between the two figures arises mainly because the periods are not the same. As the structure of the economy changes, fewer basic sector jobs are supporting more and more jobs in dependent industries; the economic base multiplier therefore rises through time, as our higher and more recent figure demonstrates.

Over shorter periods the relationship between employment change in the basic and service sectors is neither so clear, nor so

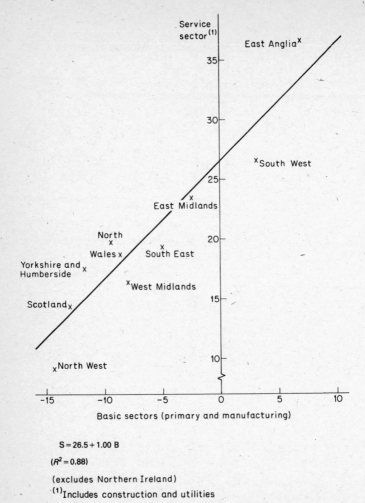

Service sector[1]

East Anglia^x

35 —

30 —

^x South West

25 —

x
East Midlands

North
x

Wales x   20 —

x
South East

Yorkshire and x
Humberside

^x West Midlands

Scotland x   15 —

10 —

x North West

-15   -10   -5   0   5   10

Basic sectors (primary and manufacturing)

$S = 26.5 + 1.00 \, B$

$(R^2 = 0.88)$

(excludes Northern Ireland)

[1] Includes construction and utilities

Figure 3.1   Employment change in the basic and service sectors by region 1952–79 (as percentage of total employment in each region in 1952)

strong. For example, between 1966 and 1979 every four per cent change in total employment arising in the basic sectors led to a change in the service sector of only three per cent, whereas the corresponding long-term relationship for 1952–79 was one-for-one. This reflects the slowness with which levels of dependent service employment adjust to new levels of basic employment in each region. Indeed, service employment in any one short period will reflect events in the immediately preceding years as well as

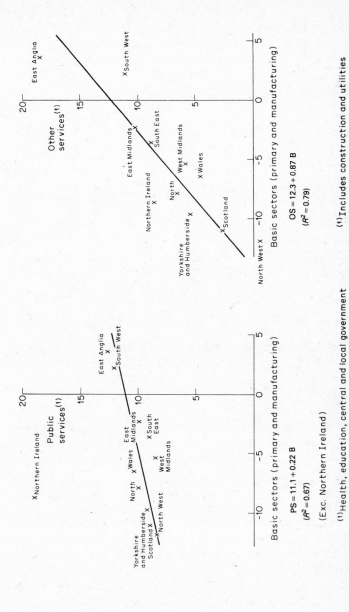

Figure 3.2 Employment change in the basic sectors and in public and other services by region 1952–75 (as percentage of 1952 total employment in each region)

changes in basic employment during the period itself. Only by taking a longer view, such as the one we have taken, is it possible to overcome these lags in the system and identify a simple and unambiguous relationship.

Employment in basic services will of course remain largely unaffected by changes in primary and manufacturing employment. Among the remainder of the service sector, public services—health, education and central and local government—have responded particularly slowly to changes in basic employment, as Figure 3.2 illustrates. To some extent this is to be expected because public service provision is closely related to the level of population, which changes only slowly in response to job opportunities in any area. However, the variation between regions in the growth of public service employment has been remarkably small—much smaller than the variation in population growth in fact—and suggests that as a matter of policy the assisted areas have been favoured in the allocation of new jobs in the public sector. This is perhaps not surprising, given that public service provision and employment are determined by political decisions rather than market forces. The best evidence is provided by Northern Ireland, which has experienced a quite remarkable growth in public service employment. This has meant that total employment in the province is now no less than ten per cent higher than it would have been if the public sector had expanded at the same rate as elsewhere. Though we have no direct evidence to explain why Northern Ireland should be so different, it is difficult not to conclude that the expansion of public services has been a response to the province's political troubles, particularly as the bulk of the increase has occurred since the late 1960s.

Northern Ireland is unusual, but illustrates the point that regional differences in service growth cannot be attributed entirely to the second-round effects of employment change in the primary and manufacturing sectors. In some regions service growth is higher than can be explained by these second-round effects, and in others lower. Moreover, at the level of individual service industries locational trends are more complex and varied, and often need to be understood in terms of the pressures upon that individual industry as well as the more general influences on service employment.

The location of growth and decline in basic services is one of the factors which weakens the link with employment change in the primary and manufacturing sectors, but two other influences are worth noting. The first is the convergence in regional levels of income. Since the mid-1960s income per head has fallen relative to the national average in those regions where it was highest, such as the South East, and risen where it was below average, notably in Scotland, Northern Ireland and the North. Because so much service employment is supported by local consumer spending, it is likely that the convergence in regional income levels has led to some differences in the growth of service employment.

The second influence is the movement of office jobs out of the South East and out of London in particular. This decentralisation comprises two separate elements: the movement of civil service jobs out of London as a deliberate act of policy, and the voluntary movement of private offices to new locations. Figures from the Civil Service Department show that 17,000 public jobs were decentralised from the South East, mainly to the assisted areas, between 1963 and 1975. Records of private office moves are incomplete because they relate only to the clients of the Location of Offices Bureau, but these show that during the same years 27,000 jobs in private offices moved out of the South East, though fewer found their way to the assisted areas. In total, the number of jobs involved in office moves from the South East represents about one per cent of all service jobs in the region. Nevertheless, these are minor qualifications to the main conclusion. At the regional scale, the evidence shows that the service sector has played a largely dependent role in unequal growth.

Service Growth in Cities and Small Towns

At the sub-regional scale the issue is not so clear-cut. One of the reasons is that in individual areas specific factors disturb the relationship between changes in basic sector employment and changes in service employment. For example, the Outer Metropolitan Area has experienced a very rapid growth in service employment, at least part of which must be attributed to the decentralisation of 'mobile' service jobs out of the capital. In addition, complex patterns of commuting, especially around the conurbations, often mean that the basic jobs in one sub-region support service jobs in another sub-region where the commuters live.

In part, the link between basic and service employment is not so strong at the sub-regional scale because service employment has not grown as quickly as might have been expected in smaller towns and rural areas. Table 3.7 shows that the contribution of service employment growth to total employment has been below average in London and the conurbations and above average elsewhere. This is a familiar picture: manufacturing growth also displays marked urban-rural contrasts, as we have seen. The similarity is to be expected since the growth of basic sector employment, including

Table 3.7 The causes of service employment change by type of area 1959–75

	Service sector[1] employment change	Change attributed to:		
		National growth	Multiplier[2]	Residual
London	+ 1.9	+10.8	−7.6	−1.3
Conurbations	+ 5.9	+10.8	−4.9	0
Free standing cities	+16.0	+10.8	+2.2	+3.0
Industrial towns	+21.1	+10.8	+6.6	+3.7
County towns	+15.2	+10.8	+8.5	−4.1
Rural areas	+11.4	+10.8	+8.6	−8.0
G.B.	+10.8	+10.8	0	0

as % 1959 total employment in each area

[1]includes construction and utilities.
[2]assumes that a gain or loss of one job in the primary or manufacturing sector, relative to the U.K. as a whole, leads to a gain or loss of one job in dependent service activities.

manufacturing, affects the growth of service employment. However, if we allow for a long-run multiplier effect of the same magnitude as that which we calculated for regions (2.0), the trends in each type of area look considerably different.

The interesting item in Table 3.7 is the 'residual', obtained after allowing for multiplier effects from the primary and manufacturing sectors, which provides a measure of 'autonomous' shifts in service employment. This shows that service employment is more or less holding its own in the largest cities, is growing in smaller cities and industrial towns, and is declining in county towns and especially in rural areas. These locational trends are hidden in aggregate figures for service employment change by the upward boost to services in small towns and rural areas provided by the growth of basic employment. Other things being equal, it seems that service jobs are drifting out of small towns and rural areas and into larger towns.

There are probably two reasons why this is happening. The first is that because cities and larger towns have traditionally acted as service centres for their hinterlands, many of the activities which have experienced the fastest growth in employment in recent years—business services, higher education and public administration, for example—are concentrated in larger settlements rather than in small towns and rural areas. The second is that over and above the influence of these rapidly growing service employers, rising car ownership has provided more small-town residents with easy access to cities so that other services, such as retailing, have gravitated towards urban centres.

The Importance of Manufacturing

The division of total employment into basic and dependent sectors has proved fruitful. It has shown that the service sector, despite its size, is of only minor importance in causing growth and decline. Services are certainly a more important employer in some areas than others, and there has been an increase in their share of total employment. Nevertheless, variations in service employment growth from place to place occur mainly because employment change in the basic sectors—agriculture, mining and manufacturing—is spread unevenly across cities and regions. There are examples contradicting this general statement, such as a town whose prosperity is based upon the growth of a local university, or a seaside resort where the fortunes of the tourist industry are crucial, but these are exceptions to the rule. Some service jobs do affect their local economies independently of what is happening in other sectors, but the point is that they form only a small part of the sector as a whole. Probably the only important qualification we need to introduce to our main conclusion—that in the long run the location of service jobs follows the location of basic jobs—is that within regions services are showing a tendency to gravitate away from small towns and rural areas. The rest of our investigation therefore need not pay much attention to services, but must concentrate on agriculture, mining and manufacturing. Employment change in these sectors is the principal motor of unequal growth.

Earlier we noted that the size of any sector's contribution to total employment change depends on two things: the proportion of total employment in that sector at the start of the period, and its subsequent rate of employment change. The role of the primary sector (agriculture and mining) is almost entirely explained by the first of these—its share of employment in each area. During the last twenty or thirty years the primary sector has been a major source of decline in those areas where it was once an important employer, such as East Anglia. Wales and the North, but the rate of decline has varied very little from place to place. For example, all regions lost between 50 and 70 per cent of their primary employment between 1952 and 1979.

This is an important point because the location of natural

resources—good agricultural land and mineral resources—largely
determines the areas in which the primary sector is an important
employer. Given that primary employment has fallen at much the
same rate in all areas, the size of the primary sector's contribution to
employment change in any area has therefore depended mainly on
the location of natural resources. Even some of the small differences
between local and national trends can be explained by natural
resource endowment. Mining employment has declined rather faster
in Wales and the North, for instance, than in the East Midlands and
Yorkshire. This reflects the location of easily workable coal reserves:
in the East Midlands and Yorkshire the seams tend to be thicker and
less faulted, so a smaller proportion of the pits have been closed.
Like the service sector, the primary sector need not therefore detain
us any further. Though it would be wrong to ignore the quite
substantial impact which the primary sector has had on the pattern
of employment change since the last war, its contribution in any
area can be explained fairly easily in terms of the location of natural
resources.

In contrast to the primary sector, the contribution of manufacturing to unequal growth depends almost entirely on variations in its
rate of growth from place to place, not on its relative importance as
an employer. No region illustrates this point better than East
Anglia, which in the early 1950s had the smallest proportion of
employment in manufacturing of any region, yet in subsequent years
the contribution of its manufacturing sector to total employment
change was the largest in any region. Indeed, Chapter 2 has already
shown the marked disparities in the rate of growth of manufacturing
employment, both between regions and within them. These
disparities play the crucial role in generating unequal growth, and
the next five chapters explain their causes.

If the only justification for focusing on manufacturing was to
resolve the many conflicting theories which purport to explain
industrial location, that would be sufficient by itself, but there is a
further reason for concentrating on manufacturing: in the 1980s it
has emerged even more clearly as the dominant influence upon
unequal growth. This is because the other basic sectors, agriculture
and mining, which played an important role in the past, have
experienced such a dramatic decline in employment that neither
now employs substantial numbers except in one or two places. By
the late 1970s the primary sector employed only three per cent of the
total workforce in Britain and, even in the areas we have classed as
'rural', agriculture employed only one in fifteen of all workers. The
decline of primary employment has slowed in recent years, but even

if it were to accelerate once more it would have little effect on most areas now that so few people depend on this sector for their livelihood. For better or worse, in a period when British manufacturing is in crisis, the pattern of urban and regional growth depends more than ever on what happens to manufacturing employment.

4 Industrial Structure

Ask any manager what are the main determinants of employment levels in his firm and he will generally pick out factors which have little to do with location. He will draw your attention to things such as the growth of the national market for his product, international competition, and the effect of technical change on the numbers of workers he needs on the shop floor. On the whole he is correct. Firms operate within the context of the national and international economy, and this profoundly affects their employment. The logic of the market place is that, in the long run, no firm can continue to produce goods which nobody will buy. Nor can firms ignore technical innovations which reduce costs and labour requirements, and thus affect competitiveness.

The most obvious way in which the national economic context in Britain has affected manufacturing employment is that the declining fortunes of the economy have led to fewer jobs everywhere. Manufacturing employment has grown more slowly—or declined faster—in every region since 1966. However, national trends affect not only the overall *level* of employment, but also the *pattern* of employment change. To put it another way, national trends determine not only how many jobs there are to share out, but also where some of these jobs are located.

The growth of the market, international competition and technical progress do not affect all industries in the same way. Changing patterns of demand mean that some industries face stagnant or contracting markets while others—computers and electronic goods for instance—benefit from growing demand even when the national economy is depressed. The share of the national market taken by imports also varies between industries, and the extent to which productivity can be raised by replacing labour with machinery depends very much on the nature of the product. Each of these influences varies in strength and direction from industry to industry, but their net effect is that employment in different industries grows at different rates. This is important because the mix of industries (or *industrial structure*) varies from area to area. In this chapter we therefore test the proposition that some areas are in decline because they have more than their fair share of industries whose employment is declining in the country as a whole, while other areas grow because they have a large share of industries in which employment is growing nationally.

Probably no other idea has had such a large impact upon how people explain 'the regional problem'. For over half a century the problems of Scotland and the North of England have been explained away as being due to high concentrations of 'old' industries—textiles, shipbuilding, and steel—which are in decline in Britain as a whole. Modern industrial development supersedes these industries by the consumer-orientated industries, such as motors and electrical engineering, which are found in the South and Midlands. This explanation for unequal growth can be found in nearly all official studies since the war. It is an analysis which has been accepted by both major political parties, and ministerial statements still draw heavily on the idea of old declining industries to justify regional assistance. In fact, as we will show, the impact of industrial structure has been much more modest than is generally assumed. Indeed, since the mid-sixties its influence on the pattern of employment change has been negligible.

But first it is important to look briefly at what is meant by a 'growing' or 'declining' industry. A point which is often overlooked is that if an industry's employment is falling, this does not necessarily mean that the demand for its products, and thus its output, is contracting. For example, since the early 1950s employment in the timber and furniture trades has fallen but their output has doubled, and even in the textile industry, which has experienced chronic job losses, output has increased by a third. In these industries the loss of jobs has occurred because productivity has risen faster than output. Likewise, similar levels of output growth can be compatible with quite different employment trends, depending on the extent to which new technology and improved management practices lead to increases in labour productivity.

Also, what is often considered as a declining industry in Britain may be experiencing growth in other countries. Steel and shipbuilding are two good examples. Until the severe world recession of the mid-1970s, both experienced strong growth in output and employment in most industrial economies. Insofar as steel and shipbuilding declined in Britain this was because they failed to maintain their share of domestic and world markets in the face of foreign competition. In contrast, employment in textiles has fallen in all the major Western economies, including Britain, as a result of cheap Third World imports. Motor vehicles and electrical engineering are particularly interesting because for most of the post-war period they were regarded in Britain as leading growth industries, even though their expansion lagged well behind that in Europe and Japan. The shortcomings of British competitiveness in these two 'growth' industries has only become obvious now that adverse trading conditions have stopped output rising. The important point is that the simplistic view—that if an industry's employment is falling the industry must be in decline—is really a long way from the truth. Falling employment may result from rising productivity, not falling output, and employment growth may disguise a weak performance compared to overseas rivals.

Measuring the Impact of Industrial Structure

Whatever the cause, national trends in employment by industry affect the urban and regional pattern of growth because the mix of industries varies from place to place. We can measure their impact using a simple method known as shift-share analysis, which calculates the employment change which would occur in a region if each of its industries grew at the same rate as in the country as a whole. This 'expected' employment change reflects both the mix of industries in the region and their national growth, and can be compared with the actual employment change in that region. More specifically, shift-share disaggregates overall employment change into three components:

1.   *A national component*, which is the change that would have occurred if total employment in an area had grown at the same rate as total employment in the country as a whole.
2.   *A structural component*, which is the change relative to the country as a whole that can be attributed to an area's particular mix of industries. This is calculated as the change which would have occurred if each industry in the area had grown at the national rate for that industry, less the national component.
3.   *A differential shift*, which is the difference between the expected change (i.e. the sum of the national and structural components) and the actual change in that area.

Shift-share is a well known and widely used method, but like all simple methods it has been much criticised (e.g., Richardson 1978). In particular, some critics have suggested that the choice of base year and the level of disaggregation at which the analysis is conducted affect the results. However, we have made an exhaustive examination of these and other criticisms (Fothergill and Gudgin 1979b) and have concluded that in the context of British regions shift-share analysis is a highly robust technique. Neither the choice of base year nor the level of disaggregation makes any substantial difference to the results.

Though there is nothing new in the use of shift-share analysis to identify the influence of industrial structure, previous studies of urban and regional employment change in Britain have generally concentrated on short periods, so that the long-term impact of industrial structure has been obscured. Table 4.1 is therefore interesting because it presents the results of a shift-share analysis of manufacturing employment change in each region for the comparatively long period from 1952 to 1979.

The first point to note is that industrial structure, measured by the structural component, has been an important influence in some regions but has had barely any impact in others. The South East has been the principal beneficiary, reflecting the large share of post-war growth industries, such as electrical engineering, found in this region. The West Midlands, too, has had a favourable structure for employment growth. The most disadvantaged regions have been those in which textiles are important employers—Yorkshire and Humberside (wool textiles), the North West (cotton) and, worst of all, Northern Ireland (linen). But in several regions industrial structure has not had a very great impact on employment change in either direction. For example, Wales and the North have often been thought of as having a 'bad' industrial structure because of their reliance on declining industries such as steel and shipbuilding. In fact, taking their manufacturing industrial structures as a whole, neither region has been badly handicapped by its inherited mix of industries. It is certainly true that the structure of employment in these regions has posed severe problems, but this has been due to their heavy reliance on the declining coal industry, not to a particularly unfavourable mix of manufacturing industries.

A second important point is that the link between actual manufacturing employment change and the favourability of a region's industrial structure is tenuous. In three declining regions— Northern Ireland, Yorkshire and Humberside and the North West—a poor industrial structure has been an important cause of decline. On the other hand, none of the five growing regions owes very much to a favourable industrial structure and, despite the best industrial structure of all, the South East has actually lost employment at a slightly faster rate than the country as a whole.

Thirdly, arising out of the last point, some of the changes in employment which cannot be attributed to industrial structure are very large indeed. Virtually all the exceptionally strong manufacturing growth in East Anglia can be attributed to other influences,

Table 4.1 Shift-share analysis of manufacturing employment change by region 1952–79

| | 1952 manufacturing employment thousands | as % 1952 employment | | |
		National component	Structural component	Differential shift	Actual change
East Anglia	138	−7.8	+ 4.1	+74.0	+70.3
South West	331	−7.8	+ 3.4	+30.1	+25.7
Wales	268	−7.8	− 1.0	+26.3	+17.5
East Midlands	534	−7.8	− 1.9	+21.1	+11.4
North	409	−7.8	− 4.4	+20.0	+ 7.8
West Midlands	1,119	−7.8	+ 7.3	− 7.3	− 7.8
South East	2,259	−7.8	+15.1	−17.2	− 9.9
Yorkshire and Humberside	863	−7.8	−13.7	+ 7.8	−13.7
Scotland	760	−7.8	− 6.8	− 3.8	−18.4
North West	1,414	−7.8	−13.2	− 3.5	−24.5
Northern Ireland	186	−7.8	−26.7	+ 7.1	−27.1
U.K.	8,285	−7.8	0	0	− 7.8

1952 base year, 77 industry disaggregation.

measured by the differential shift. The South East's favourable industrial structure has been more than offset by a large negative differential shift. Even more striking is the fact that, by 1979, manufacturing employment in each of the five growing regions (which include Wales and the North) was more than 20 per cent higher than might have been expected on the basis of their industrial structures. At the regional scale industrial structure has therefore been of some importance, but it leaves a great deal of employment change unexplained.

Shift-share can also be used to examine the extent to which industrial structure has brought about the marked urban-rural shift in manufacturing which we noted earlier. The full results of this analysis, including the figures for each individual sub-region, have been published elsewhere (Fothergill and Gudgin 1979a), but Table 4.2 summarises the results for manufacturing employment in each type of area between 1959 and 1975. They are rather dramatic: industrial structure explains none of the urban-rural shift in manufacturing employment. Indeed, the area with the best industrial structure, London, has actually experienced the worst employment losses. Moreover, the differential shift shows a very large and consistent urban-rural contrast. The larger and more industrial a settlement, the faster its differential decline. The association between settlement size and differential growth is remarkable. As Table 4.3 shows, just as London fares worse than the conurbations, even among these conurbations the largest fare worse than the smallest. The deterioration in differential growth with increasing size is evident both among those conurbations which have development area status—Clydeside, Merseyside and Tyneside—and those conurbations outside the development areas.

An interesting contrast has emerged. On the one hand industrial structure has contributed to regional growth differences, but on the other it accounts for none of the urban-rural divergence in growth. This is mainly because of the legacy of earlier periods of industrialisation in Britain. Most of the major nineteenth-century industries—shipbuilding, textiles, steel and heavy engineering—developed in Northern England, Scotland and Wales and were spread quite widely across cities and smaller towns within these regions, largely because of the local availability of coal as a source of power. In the early twentieth century the new consumer industries also showed a 'regional' pattern of location, but this time it was the South and Midlands which benefited. As a result Britain has a pattern of industrial location which differentiates broad areas of the

Table 4.2 Shift-share analysis of manufacturing employment change by type of area 1959–75

	1959 manufacturing employment thousands	as % 1959 employment			
		National component	Structural component	Differential shift	Actual change
London	1,551	−5.3	+8.3	−40.8	−37.8
Conurbations	2,734	−5.3	−4.2	− 6.3	−15.9
Free standing cities	1,647	−5.3	+1.0	+ 9.1	+ 4.8
Industrial towns	1,568	−5.3	−0.4	+21.9	+16.3
County towns	640	−5.3	+1.3	+32.8	+28.8
Rural areas	95	−5.3	−1.6	+84.1	+77.2
G.B.	8,234	−5.3	+0.4[1]	−0.3[1]	−5.2

1959 base year, 99 industry disaggregation.
[1] do not add to zero because of exclusion of Northern Ireland.

Table 4.3 Differential shifts in manufacturing employment in the conurbations
1959-75

	1959 manufacturing employment thousands	Differential shift as % 1959 man. emp.
Non-development areas		
London	1,551	−40.8
Birmingham	716	−18.6
Manchester	597	− 8.3
West Yorkshire	464	+ 2.1
Development areas		
Clydeside	454	− 6.2
Merseyside	276	+ 1.7
Tyneside	227	+10.3

1959 base year, 99 industry disaggregation.

country, such as whole regions, rather than one which differentiates, within any region, between cities, towns and rural areas. In other countries, where the history of economic growth has produced a different pattern of industrial location, the role of industrial structure in generating unevenness in employment is of course likely to be rather different to that found in Britain.

The Declining Role of Industrial Structure

An important aspect of the role of industrial structure in regional growth is that its influence has been uneven through time. This is demonstrated by Figure 4.1 which shows the structural component by region between 1952 and 1979, but this time including three intermediate dates. In this diagram the structural component has been calculated throughout the whole period using the 1952 mix of industries in each region, but an almost identical pattern emerges even if an allowance is made for the changing mix of industries in each region (by using 1960 as the base year for 1960-6, 1966 as the base year for 1966-73, and 1973 for 1973-9).

Up to 1966 industrial structure was responsible for quite large disparities in growth, but thereafter its influence has been much more modest. The loss of employment due to an adverse structure in Northern Ireland, the North West, Scotland and the North eased substantially after 1966. The growth due to a favourable industrial

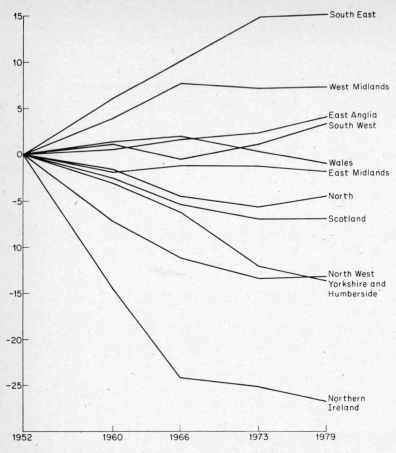

Figure 4.1   The structural component by region 1952–79 (as percentage of 1952 manufacturing employment)

structure in the West Midlands stopped after 1966, and since 1973 even the high-flying South East has not benefited from its mix of industries. So despite its continuing popularity as an explanation for regional growth and decline, industrial structure has in fact become more or less irrelevant.

The extent to which a region's industrial structure favours employment growth depends on two factors: firstly, the mix of industries in that region at the start of the period, and secondly the subsequent national employment change in each of those industries. In theory, the demise of industrial structure as an important influence on regional growth could be the result of either or both of these factors. Certainly, there has been a tendency for the mix of industries in each region to grow more alike. However, in Figure 4.1 the mix of industries has been held constant (as at 1952) and, as we noted, the same pattern emerges even using the mix of industries of other years. The conclusion must therefore be that the demise of industrial structure has been entirely the result of changes in national employment trends in individual industries.

It is not difficult to explain why this has happened. During the years in which U.K. manufacturing employment was rising there were large disparities between growing and declining industries. Between 1952 and 1966 the fastest-growing third expanded their employment by an average of 36 per cent, while the slowest-growing third lost 21 per cent. Because the share of employment in these growing and declining industries varied from region to region, industrial structure accounted for quite large differences in growth during these years. After 1966, as national decline set in, industrial growth rates became much more alike, and nearly all in a downward direction. The worst third lost 34 per cent of their employment between 1966 and 1979, but even the best third lost 3 per cent—a much smaller gap between top and bottom. As industrial growth rates became more alike their tendency to generate regional disparities diminished.

The West Midlands illustrates this process. Up to 1966 its industrial structure was favoured by national trends, but not thereafter. This change in the structural trend meant that by 1979 the region had about 8 per cent, or 80,000, fewer manufacturing jobs than it would have had if national trends had continued to favour it in the same way as they had done up to 1966. The turn-around is almost wholly explained by the fortunes of the motor industry, which employs around one in six of the region's manufacturing workers. Up to 1966 the motor industry was one of Britain's leading growth industries, expanding its employment considerably faster than the manufacturing sector as a whole. After 1966, national employment in the motor industry fell, as in so many other manufacturing industries, and its growth (or rather its rate of decline) ceased to be very much better than the rest of Britain's manufacturing sector, with the consequence that the West Midland's industrial structure became distinctly less favourable. Indeed, in the 1980s motor vehicle production has become one of Britain's most vulnerable industries, with the possibility of an even faster decline in employment than in the rest of manufacturing. If this happens, then it is likely that the West Midlands industrial structure will become unfavourable for employment growth.

Recent research at the Department of Applied Economics in

Cambridge (so far unpublished) has looked more closely at how national trends in each industry have affected each region. In particular this research has examined the extent to which the remaining structural handicaps faced by some regions since 1966 are the result of import penetration in certain sectors of the economy. The surprising conclusion is that changes in Britain's overseas trade have not disadvantaged any one region much more than any other. Insofar as the industrial structure in some regions has been a handicap, this has resulted from slow growth in the national market for certain products or from job losses associated with rapid increases in labour productivity. Nevertheless, while import penetration has not brought about *disparities* in regional employment change, it cannot be denied that it has reduced *levels* of employment in all areas.

The Changing Mix of Industries

It is still worth looking briefly at the separate role played by the changing mix of industries in each region. Thirty years of industrial development have altered the balance between industries in the economy as a whole and in local areas, so it is likely that there have been some changes in the extent to which the mix of industries in each region favours or handicaps employment growth. We have tackled this question by looking at the period from 1973 to 1979, the years of severe recession following the 1973 oil crisis. The influence of industrial structure in each region during these years has first been calculated using the mix of industries in 1973, and then recalculated, but this time using the 1952 mix of industries in each region. In this way it is possible to see the extent to which, by 1973, each region's mix of industries was better or worse for employment growth (relative to the rest of Britain) than it had been at the start of the 1950s.

The most noticeable feature of Table 4.4, which presents the results, is the small impact of industrial structure during these years—something we have already noted—but what is also striking is the minor effect of changes in industrial structure. On the whole, the favourability of each region's mix of industries altered very little between 1952 and 1973. Moreover, the small changes which have occurred are surprising. By 1973 the industrial structures of the four development area regions (Scotland, Wales, Northern Ireland and the North) were actually less favourable than in the early 1950s, despite the large number of branch plants which moved into these regions in the intervening years.

This is a sad comment on regional policy, which apart from

Table 4.4 *The influence of industrial structure on manufacturing employment change 1973–9*

	as % 1973 manufacturing employment	
	calculated using 1952 industrial structure[1]	calculated using 1973 industrial structure[1]
East Anglia	+1.0	+1.8
South West	+0.8	+1.4
South East	+0.4	+1.5
West Midlands	+0.4	+0.6
North West	+0.3	−0.5
North	+0.2	−0.4
Scotland	+0.1	−0.3
Northern Ireland	−0.9	−4.3
Wales	−1.0	−1.3
East Midlands	−1.1	−1.2
Yorkshire & Humberside	−1.5	−2.5

[1]structural component of a shift-share analysis for 1952–79 minus the structural component for 1952–73, using 1952 base year and 77 industry disaggregation.
[2]structural component of a shift-share analysis for 1973–79, using 1973 base year and 77 industry disaggregation.

providing jobs in the short run has aimed to improve the industrial structure of the assisted areas so as to provide a basis for long-run self-sustaining growth. Clearly it has failed in the latter aim. What has in fact happened is that many of the 'growth' industries which regional policy diverted to the assisted areas in the 1960s, such as electrical engineering and motor vehicles, have subsequently begun to decline like the rest of British manufacturing, and have therefore not led to any improvement in the industrial structure in these areas. On the other hand, too much weight should not be placed upon the small changes shown in Table 4.4. The important point is really that, since the early 1970s, industrial structure has become more or less irrelevant as an explanation for disparities in regional growth.

But what about the future? Could there be a resurgence in the importance of industrial structure in regional growth? Probably not. Many of the industries which were formerly major employers, and heavily concentrated in one or two regions, have declined to the extent that they are no longer such important employers in their regions. These industries include cotton, wool textiles, linen, shipbuilding and footwear. In the North West for example, cotton employed 265,000 people in 1952, but fewer than 50,000 in 1980. A further decline in industries such as these would no longer have quite the same dire consequences on manufacturing employment levels in the regions where they are located. One or two regions remain heavily dependent on just a few industries, such as steel in

Wales and motors in the West Midlands, but these are the exception rather than the rule. What is more, no new regional concentrations of individual manufacturing industries have emerged. Some of the post-war growth industries, such as electrical engineering, have become quite dispersed, at least partly because regional policy has diverted many branch plants into areas where these industries had previously not existed. If these post-war growth industries subsequently become the declining parts of British manufacturing they are therefore unlikely to handicap any one region too severely.

Other Shifts in Employment

Industrial structure alone does not provide an adequate explanation for disparities in employment change. Furthermore, as we have shown, the role of industrial structure has diminished through time. It is therefore appropriate to take a closer look at the residual disparities in growth, or differential shifts as they are known. These were measured in the shift-share analyses by the difference between the actual employment change in each area and the employment change which could be expected on the basis of its industrial structure. In fact, differential shifts subsume several separate and sometimes conflicting influences on the location of employment change, but at this stage they are worth looking at because they can be useful, in our subsequent analysis, in helping to identify the underlying causes.

Figure 4.2 shows the differential shift in manufacturing employment through time for each region. In some regions the trend has been unbroken since the early 1950s. East Anglia, the South West and East Midlands have fared well throughout the period, while there has been a slow but steady differential decline in the North West and West Midlands. Clearly, the factors underlying the persistent differential growth or decline in these regions must be remarkably consistent. In other regions there have been changes in trends. Wales, the North, Yorkshire and Humberside, Scotland and Northern Ireland all improved in the 1960s, and there was a corresponding deterioration in the South East. After 1973 trends in these regions changed once more. The differential growth of Wales and the North has come to an end, and Northern Ireland has declined very sharply, while the South East continues to decline but at a slower rate. As will be seen later, some of these changes in trends owe a great deal to regional policy.

Evidence examined later, in Chapter 7, suggests that the differential shift out of large cities and into small towns and rural areas accelerated sharply at the end of the 1950s. Subsequently the

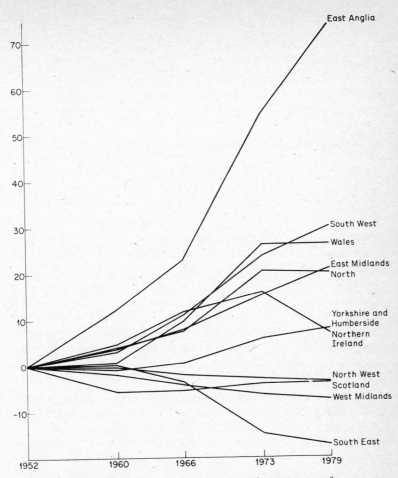

Figure 4.2 Differential shifts by region 1952–79 (as percentage of 1952 manufacturing employment)

shift proceeded at a rapid rate during each of the three periods shown in Table 4.5, though the figures indicate that it slowed slightly in the 1970s. If London and the six conurbations are taken together, their negative differential shift averaged 56,000 jobs a year in the early 1960s, 51,000 in the late 1960s, and 40,000 in the early 1970s. The differential shift, representing employment change after allowing for the impact of industrial structure, is the best measure of decentralisation from the cities because it shows 'autonomous' shifts in industrial location. Contrary to popular opinion, therefore, it seems that the 1960s rather than the 1970s were the period when the decentralisation of manufacturing employment from the big cities

Table 4.5 Differential shifts in manufacturing employment by type of area and period

	thousand per year[1]		
	1959–66	1966–71	1971–75
London	−40	−47	−30
Conurbations	−16	− 4	−10
Free standing cities	+10	+16	0
Industrial towns	+27	+13	+22
County towns	+12	+16	+11
Rural areas	+ 5	+ 4	+ 6

1959 base year, 99 industry disaggregation.
[1] do not add to zero because of exclusion of Northern Ireland.

was proceeding at its most rapid rate. When suitable data becomes available for the late 1970s it will be important to see whether this slowing in decentralisation has continued.

For the period 1952 to 1975, we have been able to examine differential shifts in individual industries, though only at the regional scale. This is very useful because, if differential shifts are consistent across all industries in a region, then the explanation for this must be that there are pervasive locational influences affecting industrial growth in that region. If differential shifts are dominated by only one or two industries, however, the explanation is more likely to be specific to those industries. At the level of individual industries there is considerable diversity within each region, in both the strength and direction of differential shifts, but much of this is random, especially in some of the industries which employ few people. Despite the diversity, most industries in each region mirror the differential shift in the region as a whole. Thus in each of the five regions where there was a strongly favourable differential shift— East Anglia, Wales, the South West, North and East Midlands— employment in roughly three-quarters of the industries grew faster than the national average for those industries. In the South East, where the overall shift was strongly negative, three-quarters of the industries experienced below average growth. Whatever it is that is responsible for the good or bad performance in some regions it must therefore be something which affects a wide range of industries. Nevertheless, the largest differences in growth tend to be concentrated in the faster-growing industries, as Table 4.6 illustrates. The faster the national growth of employment in an industry, the greater the disparity in its growth between regions. Conversely, industries which have been shedding jobs rapidly have done so in most regions,

Table 4.6   Differential shifts in fast and slow growing manufacturing industries 1952–75

Industry growth[1]	Differential shift as % 1952 employment in each group of industries in each region	
	Growing regions[2]	Declining regions
Fast (+20% or more)	+56.3	−15.6
Medium	+17.4	− 8.3
Slow (−20% or more)	+ 6.2	− 4.1

1952 base year, 77 industry disaggregation.
[1]U.K. employment change 1952–75.
[2]regions with an overall positive differential shift in manufacturing, i.e. East Anglia, South West, Wales, North, East Midlands, Northern Ireland, Yorkshire and Humberside.

consequently contributing little to differential shifts between regions.

The importance of growing industries in determining the regional pattern of employment change is demonstrated by electrical engineering, which expanded its employment substantially over the period as a whole. In the South East this industry accounts for a negative differential shift of nearly 100,000 jobs, that is, more than one-quarter of the region's total negative shift. Electrical engineering also shows one of the largest positive differential shifts in Scotland, Wales, Northern Ireland and the North, where regional incentives have attracted new branch plants away from the South East, and it has been important in the growth of the South West and East Midlands. The motor industry—another growth industry, over the post-war period as a whole—also accounts for some large differential shifts, particularly associated with diversion of growth generated in the West Midlands into new branch plants in Merseyside and Central Scotland.

The evidence therefore suggests that after allowing for the influence of industrial structure, the remaining shifts in employment are more the result of the location of new jobs in growing industries than they are due to the location of job losses in declining industries. To put it another way, the location of new factories and the expansion of existing ones are probably more important than the location of contractions and closures. This conclusion is confirmed later when we look at shifts in employment using firm-by-firm information.

The Second-Round Effects of Industrial Structure

One possibility that has not been considered so far is that differential shifts in employment might be no more than the 'second-round' effects of industrial structure. When a major industry declines it reduces the business available to its local suppliers, especially if that industry is one, such as shipbuilding or motor vehicles, which really does little more than assemble bought-in components. Thus the problems of Clydeside and Tyneside, for instance, might in theory all be attributable to the decline of shipbuilding. When the shipyards closed, they took with them a whole host of local marine engineering, fabrication and sub-contracting firms. And the problem does not stop there. Because old staple industries have disappeared, local incomes are lower, and therefore local consumer-oriented manufacturing industries, like baking and brewing, go downhill too.

The importance of these second-round effects of industrial structure has, however, been vastly exaggerated. Even if they were very large indeed they could not explain the pattern of differential shifts which can be observed. We have already noted that there have been huge differential shifts out of the cities and into smaller towns and rural areas, yet the effect of industrial structure has been broadly neutral over this urban-rural spectrum. Moreover, at the regional scale the effect of industrial structure in boosting or lowering employment has often been in the *opposite* direction to the differential shift. The South East is the best example here: despite the most favourable industrial structure, it has experienced the worst differential growth. Furthermore, even when the influence of industrial structure and the differential shift run in the same direction, as in East Anglia, the differential shift can be many times larger.

The second-round or 'multiplier' effects of industrial structure may still be important in one or two places, so it is worth attempting to quantify them. There is a good case for taking a close look at Scotland, and we are fortunate in that the availability of detailed information makes this task easier. Scotland possesses a disproportionately large number of jobs in shipbuilding and textiles, two declining industries, and in total its poor industrial structure caused the loss of 50,000 jobs relative to the U.K. between 1952 and 1979. At the same time, and despite regional aid, Scotland lost an additional 30,000 jobs because of the weak performance of its manufacturing sector (measured by the differential shift). It seems likely that at least some of the poor performance of Scottish manufacturing is due to multiplier effects from its poor industrial structure.

The second-round impact of Scotland's poor industrial structure can be investigated using the 'input-output' tables which have been produced for this region in 1973 (Fraser of Allander Institute 1978). These are based on answers to a survey carried out among the region's firms (in all sectors of the economy), asking them from whom, and where, they obtained their raw materials and other inputs, and to whom they sold their output. The information obtained was used to assemble a highly detailed picture of the sales and purchases of different industries, including the transactions within the Scottish manufacturing sector itself. The input-output tables, backed up by a few simple assumptions, may be used to estimate the second-round effect, via these 'industrial linkages', of the decline of Scotland's traditional old-established industries.

The conclusion which emerges is surprising at first sight. Despite Scotland's reliance on declining industries such as shipbuilding, the region's adverse industrial structure has had a negligible second-round effect on other industries via industrial linkages. The reason is not hard to find: Scotland, like all the other U.K. regions, is a very 'open' economy in which only about ten per cent of its manufacturing employment is dependent on the purchases of other Scottish manufacturing industries. The impact of industrial linkages within Scottish manufacturing—and probably elsewhere too—has therefore been small. But this is only part of the story. Though only ten per cent of the region's manufacturing jobs are dependent on linkages, if we include the manufacturing jobs dependent on *all* Scottish markets—consumers, the public sector, and non-manufacturing firms, as well as manufacturing itself—then the proportion rises to a third.

At this point it is useful to return to a distinction introduced earlier, between basic and dependent industries. Previously we have used these categories to differentiate the primary and manufacturing industries, which are mainly basic and bring income into an area, from services which are mainly dependent and rely on local population and markets. At the time we noted that the allocation of whole sectors to these headings was simplistic, even if not too wide of the mark. In fact, the Scottish input-output tables show that about one-third of the region's manufacturing is dependent on local markets, while a small proportion of the Scottish service sector is basic, in that it is supported by demand from outside the region.

Taking the Scottish economy as a whole, for every eight basic jobs in manufacturing there are two basic service jobs, and four further dependent jobs in manufacturing. This is important because it means that for every ten basic jobs lost, we would expect, *in the long*

Table 4.7   The second-round effect of industrial structure on manufacturing differential shifts by region 1952—79

	Differential shift as % 1952 manufacturing employment	
	Before deducting second-round effect of industrial structure	After deducting second-round effect of industrial structure
East Anglia	+74	+73
South West	+30	+29
Wales	+26	+27
East Midlands	+21	+22
North	+20	+22
Yorkshire and Humberside	+ 8	+13
Northern Ireland	+ 7	+16
North West	− 4	+ 1
Scotland	− 4	− 1
West Midlands	− 7	−10
South East	−17	−22

1952 base year, 77 industry disaggregation.

run, a further four manufacturing jobs to disappear because of second-round effects. The adjustment will occur partly by reducing the demand for locally manufactured inputs for basic industries, partly through a reduction in local incomes and partly because a fall in basic employment will encourage out-migration. The last of these adjustment processes—a loss of population and the consequent contraction in local markets—will of course take a long time to work itself out to its full extent.

Scotland's manufacturing sector is probably more dependent on local demand than most, because of the region's physical isolation from the rest of the U.K. and because the relatively large size of its manufacturing sector means that more firms will be able to find appropriate suppliers locally. Consequently, the second-round effect of a loss of basic jobs is unlikely to be quite as large in other regions. In Table 4.7 we have therefore assumed that for every 10 jobs gained or lost as a result of industrial structure in each region, a further 3.5 jobs have been gained or lost because of multiplier effects. This is inevitably a rough-and-ready estimate of the size of multiplier effects from industrial structure, but the table shows that they make little difference to either the size or the direction of regional differential shifts. The performances of Yorkshire and Humberside, Northern Ireland and the North West appear a little better, and that of the

South East rather worse, but the overall pattern remains virtually unchanged.

Conclusion

The influence of industrial structure has been nothing like as pervasive as is often supposed. In some areas it has certainly been important, in others not at all. It has caused some regions to grow faster than others, but at the same time it fails to explain why small towns and rural areas are growing at the expense of cities. The impact of industrial structure has also diminished over the years, though almost entirely because of the changing fortunes of different industries in the economy as a whole, rather than any dramatic convergence in the mix of industries located in each region. Indeed, industrial structure is now little more than a minor cause of disparities between local and national employment trends. In subsequent chapters we must therefore look at other factors if we are to understand the pattern of change which is now occurring.

HAROLD BRIDGES LIBRARY
S. MARTIN'S COLLEGE
LANCASTER

5 Urban Decline and Rural Resurgence

The decline of cities and growth of small towns and rural areas is the dominant aspect of change in the location of manufacturing industry in Britain and other Western industrial economies. The strength and pervasiveness of this urban-rural shift has been remarkable, and there is every prospect of it continuing. Chapter 2 showed that the contrast in manufacturing employment change between cities and small towns has been very large—much larger than the differences between regions—and very consistent. The larger and more industrial a settlement, the faster its decline. At the two extremes, London lost nearly 40 per cent of its manufacturing jobs between 1959 and 1975, while the most rural areas increased theirs by nearly 80 per cent during the same period. Chapter 4 showed that none of this dramatic urban-rural shift can be explained by industrial structure.

Because the mix of cities, towns and rural areas—or *urban structure* as we have called it—varies so much from area to area, the urban-rural shift has a profound impact upon the pattern of employment change. This chapter examines the urban-rural shift in three stages. The first part looks more closely at its importance, and in particular at how it is the main factor bringing about shifts between regions as well as within them. Secondly, we look at the mechanisms through which the shift is brought about—the opening, closure, growth and movement of firms—and at the sorts of firms which are declining in cities and growing elsewhere. And finally, this evidence is assessed against the competing explanations for the urban-rural shift. The explanation which is best able to fit the evidence turns out to be surprisingly simple: manufacturing is in decline in the cities because a higher proportion of firms in cities are in 'constrained locations', restricted by old-fashioned premises, hemmed in by existing urban development and with no room for expansion. This means that in cities investment in machinery displaces labour on the shop floor, and thus reduces employment. The same displacement of labour from existing floorspace occurs in small towns and rural areas of course, but the greater room for expansion also allows investment in factory extensions and the construction of new factories on greenfield sites, and this is more than sufficient to produce a net increase in employment in these locations.

The Importance of Urban Structure

Some regions are markedly more urban than others. In the North West for example, roughly 60 per cent of the population are in towns of more than 100,000 people, whereas in East Anglia the proportion is only 15 per cent. The consequence is that as manufacturing shifts from urban to rural areas, some whole regions benefit at the expense of others. This is a crucial point. Put in simple terms it means that the North West does badly because it contains two conurbations (Manchester and Merseyside) while East Anglia gains because it is much more rural in character. The more a region is dominated by large urban agglomerations, the more likely it is to decline. But just how much of the regional disparities in growth can be accounted for by urban structure? More precisely, how much of the regional disparities which are not due to industrial structure—the differential shifts—can be accounted for by the strong shift in manufacturing from urban to rural areas? It is possible to answer this question using a very simple method.

We have previously grouped all sub-regions in Great Britain into one of six types on the basis of their degree of urbanisation and industrialisation. For each region it is possible to calculate the employment change which would have occurred if each sub-region within that region had grown at the average for its type. An example should make the method clearer. Let us assume that the average growth for conurbations is 8 per cent and the average growth for rural areas is 12 per cent. If a region has 75 per cent of its employment in conurbations and 25 per cent in rural areas, then its predicted growth would be:

$$(0.75 \times 8\%) + (0.25 \times 12\%) = 9\%.$$

This prediction can be compared with the actual rate of growth in that region.

We have calculated the predicted differential shift for each region assuming that each sub-region grows at the average rate for its type, except for London and the conurbations, whose predicted differential growth rates have been estimated individually using a regression line between size and differential growth in these areas. The full results of this analysis have been presented elsewhere (Fothergill and Gudgin 1979a). Figure 5.1 shows the relationship between the

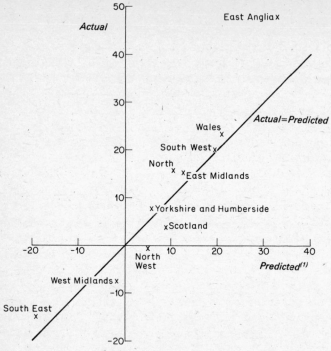

(1) Predicted on the basis of the urban structure of each region

Figure 5.1 The influence of urban structure on manufacturing differential shifts by region 1959–75 (as percentage of 1959 manufacturing employment)

actual and predicted differential shifts for each region (except Northern Ireland) between 1959 and 1975. The relationship is striking: the largest part of the variation in regional differential growth can be accounted for by the mix of urban and rural areas within each region.

The influence of the urban-rural shift in industrial location explains many important differences between regions, and in particular why areas treated similarly by government regional policy experience marked contrasts in growth. For example, though the East and West Midlands are both non-assisted regions, manufacturing growth has been much poorer in the West Midlands, a region dominated by a declining conurbation, than in the East Midlands, where industry is located in the sorts of smaller cities, towns and rural areas which have shown so much better growth in all parts of the country. Similarly, the urban-rural shift explains why Scotland, with half of its manufacturing jobs concentrated in

Clydeside, has done so much worse than Wales, even though both regions have had development area status.

Urban structure does not of course explain all the variation in regional differential growth: East Anglia, the South East and the North have fared rather better than expected, and Scotland, the North West and West Midlands rather worse. Partly this reflects the crudity of the method we have used to measure the impact of urban-rural shifts (particularly the simplicity of the grouping sub-regions into 'types of area') and partly some of the unexplained variation represents the effect of the two other influences on growth, regional policy and size structure, which are considered in later chapters. But the main point is that the shift of manufacturing from urban to rural areas is not only changing the pattern of industrial location within regions, but is also the main influence on growth differences between whole regions.

Britain is not alone in this respect. Table 5.1 compares the 'urban' and 'rural' regions in France, West Germany and Italy. Though the periods which the figures cover are considerably shorter than that which we looked at for Britain, the conclusions do not differ. In each of these countries there is a shift of manufacturing jobs from regions dominated by large cities into more rural regions, and in each country the shift has resulted from disparities in differential growth. The similarity between France, West Germany, Italy and Britain is all the more striking because of the contrasting national economic circumstances in these countries, and in particular because the growth of British manufacturing output has been much slower than in the rest of Western Europe. This evidence is important because it

Table 5.1   *Manufacturing employment change in France, West Germany and Italy*

	as % base year manufacturing employment	
	Actual change	Differential shift
France 1968–74		
Urban regions	+ 4.7	−5.9
Rural regions	+14.6	+5.5
West Germany 1970–6		
Urban regions	−16.1	−2.4
Rural regions	−13.7	+1.6
Italy 1970–4		
Urban regions	+ 2.1	−1.9
Rural regions	+ 3.3	+2.1

Urban and rural regions are defined in Appendix B.
Source: Department of Applied Economics, Cambridge.

suggests that the urban-rural shift, and its consequences for the regional pattern of growth, is probably endemic in Western industrial economies, rather than simply a feature of Britain's economic decline.

The strength and pervasiveness of the shift of manufacturing jobs from cities to small towns and rural areas indicate the pressing need for an adequate explanation, but at present there is no consensus among politicians or academics as to the cause of the problem in urban areas. The major difficulty is that the evidence which has been available to date is conflicting, patchy and unconvincing, so at this stage it is important to present some new information on the nature of the urban-rural shift. Once this evidence has been set out, it becomes much easier to make a proper evaluation of the alternative theories of urban decline. The first thing worth looking at is the way in which the urban-rural shift is being brought about—the role of openings, closures, growth and the movement of firms.

The Role of Industrial Movement

A popular view is that the decline of cities is occurring because firms are moving out. Firms based in big cities, and especially the inner city, find it difficult to operate in these locations, and managers prefer to live in the countryside anyway, so businesses are moving out to greener pastures in the commuter belt and beyond, or so the story goes. Certainly some firms behave in this way, but their contribution to the decline of the cities has been overstated.

Fortunately, the Department of Industry has collected information on the movement of firms during the post-war period. The Department uses a generous definition of industrial movement which includes both 'complete transfers' (in the sense of closing down in one location and opening up in another) and the 'movement of new branches'. If a London firm, for example, decides that rather than expand its existing factory it will instead set up a new branch plant in Norfolk, the Department defines the new branch as a move of jobs out of London and into Norfolk. In terms of the number of jobs involved, new branches are substantially more important than complete transfers. We have used the Department of Industry's movement data to produce estimates of industrial movement for each type of area between 1959 and 1975. Certain adjustments have been necessary to derive these figures, which are described in Appendix A.

Table 5.2 shows the contribution of net industrial movement (i.e., moves-in less moves-out) to the differential decline of cities and the

Table 5.2   Sources of manufacturing differential shifts by type of area 1959–75

	as % 1959 manufacturing employment		
	Industrial[1] movement	Indigenous performance	Differential[2] shift
London	−12.1	−28.7	−40.8
Conurbations	+ 1.5	− 7.8	− 6.3
Free standing cities	+ 1.1	+ 7.9	+ 9.1
Industrial towns	+ 4.2	+17.7	+21.9
County towns	+ 7.3	+25.5	+32.8
Rural areas	+29.4	+54.7	+84.1

[1] estimates based on Department of Industry figures.
[2] 1959 base year, 99 industry disaggregation.

growth of rural areas. As might be expected, London has experienced net movement out, and more rural areas (especially the most rural) have benefited from movement in, but the pattern of industrial movement can only explain at best about a third of the urban-rural shift. In London, for example, movement has led to a 12 per cent loss in employment, or around 190,000 jobs, but the weak residual performance of London's manufacturing firms has accounted for a much bigger loss of nearly 450,000 jobs.

We have called the residual shift 'indigenous performance'. This is the variation in employment change which cannot be attributed to industrial structure or industrial movement. In the main it reflects how the firms present in each area at the start of the period fared, compared to their competitors in the same industry in other areas, and to a lesser extent it also reflects contrasts in rates of new-firm formation. This definition of indigenous industry can of course include both local and non-locally owned firms. As Table 5.2 shows, indigenous performance shows a very strong and consistent contrast between urban and rural areas: the more rural an area the better the performance of its manufacturing plants.

Arguably, the table underestimates the importance of industrial movement. It has frequently been suggested that the firms which move are more dynamic than average, with prospects of longer-term growth. Indeed, Keeble (1976) found that among a sample of mobile and non-mobile firms in north-west London, the mobile firms experienced substantially better growth. Thus movement-in during one period will not only boost employment during that period but will also lead to better than average growth subsequently. Furthermore, just as an adverse industrial structure will have a second-round effect which will lower employment still further, so the

movement of firms into an area can be expected to have a
second-round effect which will further boost employment. Variations in indigenous performance might therefore be no more than
the result of the pattern of movement in earlier years. This is
unlikely, however, for the three reasons explained below.

Firstly, the magnitude of the boost given to growth by movement
in earlier periods would have to be improbably large. Even over a
sixteen-year period during which there was a great deal of industrial
movement, the variation in indigenous performance was at least
twice as large as the variation in industrial movement. Moreover,
data presented by Atkins (1973) shows that once employment in
new branch plants has reached 'mature' levels (which normally
takes seven or eight years) their growth slackens considerably.
Atkins's study, covering employment change between 1966 and
1971 in all branches which moved between 1945 and 1960, reveals
that these branches lost jobs at much the same rate as U.K.
manufacturing as a whole during these years. Employment growth
in complete transfers, however, may not slow as much as in new
branches. When a firm opens a new branch plant it generally has a
'target' employment in mind, but when a firm transfers its entire
operations from one location to another this is unlikely to be the
case. Small towns and rural areas in East Anglia, the South East,
and parts of the South West have benefited over the years from
complete transfers out of London, and in the long run this has
probably raised the indigenous performance in these areas. Nevertheless, complete transfers represent a minority of employment in all
moves, taking the country as a whole.

The second reason is that the variation in indigenous performance
probably owes little to the second-round effects of industrial
movement. Again, this is because the variation in indigenous
performance is so much larger. In the previous chapter we argued,
on the basis of evidence from Scotland, that for every ten jobs lost
due to an adverse industrial structure, in the long run a further three
or four jobs are likely to be lost due to second-round effects.
Assuming the second-round effect of movement is of much the same
magnitude—and it may be smaller because migrant plants are often
poorly integrated into their local economies—then this can only
account for a small proportion of the variation in indigenous
performance.

Finally, at the level of individual sub-regions industrial movement
and indigenous performance often act in *opposite* directions.
Clydeside is a good example. Throughout the post-war period it has
received a steady inflow of jobs in moves, mainly due to regional

policy, yet its indigenous performance remains stubbornly negative. Clydeside, and other places like it, make it difficult to explain the pattern of indigenous performance in terms of the pattern of movement.

The largest part of the shift from urban to rural areas therefore has little to do with industrial movement. Cities are declining because their plants and firms are doing worse than their competitors elsewhere. It is still possible, of course, that multi-plant companies may be shifting their operations between *existing* factories in such a way as to run down their activities in the cities, but later in the chapter we show that this form of 'disguised movement' is also of only limited importance.

The Components of Change: Evidence from One Region

We now need to examine the other 'components of change'—the opening, closure and growth of manufacturing establishments—but unfortunately this is extremely difficult. Though the Department of Industry collects information on movement, statistics on the other components of change are nothing like as comprehensive and are often non-existent. The main problem is that in order to assemble an accurate picture one requires information which covers the entire population of manufacturing establishments, from the one-man enterprise in a garden shed right through to the multi-nationals. Without such information it is impossible, for example, to measure new-firm formation. Moreover, though only a hundred or so firms account for a large proportion of total manufacturing employment, the vast majority of manufacturing firms are very small, employing perhaps only ten or twenty people, so that the task of monitoring the opening, growth and closure of firms becomes extremely arduous.

Over a number of years we have assembled a data bank for one region, the East Midlands, containing information on each of 10,000 individual manufacturing establishments. This information is based originally on the records of the Factory Inspectorate, but has been extensively augmented and improved, and covers all establishments, including the very smallest, operating in the region in 1968 and 1975. For one part of the region, Leicestershire, the records go back to 1947. For each establishment we have details of employment at different points in time, industry, location and corporate status (including ownership and control). The records have also been organised to allow us to examine the role of openings, closures, movement and the growth of surviving establishments. A fuller description of the data bank is contained in Appendix A.

The East Midlands

That our data cover only one region is not ideal, but this is not as serious a problem as it first appears, because we know a great deal about how the East Midlands compares with other regions. The influence of industrial structure has been broadly neutral (see Chapter 4) and the modest number of jobs in moves into or out of the region are roughly in balance. Insofar as the region experiences better than average manufacturing growth this is mainly because it lacks a large declining conurbation. Indeed, as we showed earlier in this chapter, the urban structure of the region explains nearly all its healthy growth. In other words, there is nothing special or unusual which is responsible for the East Midlands' relative prosperity.

From the point of view of our current concern, the important feature of the East Midlands is that it shows typical urban-rural contrasts in growth. The region's three main cities, Nottingham, Derby and Leicester, are losing jobs at much the same rate as similar cities elsewhere—places like Teesside, Bristol, Stoke and Edinburgh. In contrast, the eastern rural half of the region is experiencing the sort of steady growth typical of similar areas elsewhere in the country. Table 5.3 illustrates this point very well. Here we have grouped the local authority districts in the region into four types—cities, larger towns, smaller towns and rural areas. Even over a period as short as seven years the urban-rural contrast in employment change has been very marked and very consistent. Moreover, the shift from urban to rural areas within this region has, as elsewhere, been almost entirely due to differential shifts, not to industrial structure. Therefore by examining the components of employment change in urban and rural areas in the East Midlands it should be possible to move towards a better understanding of urban-rural shifts in the country as a whole.

The components of employment change in the four types of area in the East Midlands and in the region as a whole are shown in Table 5.4. This is an important table which is worth describing in detail. Starting with the figures for the regions as a whole, one is struck by the massive size of the job gains and job losses which are hidden by a small net change in employment. Between 1968 and 1975 a little over a quarter of all manufacturing jobs in the region (around 150,000 jobs) were lost through closures and contractions, yet these were almost entirely offset by gains from other sources, so that the net decline in employment was very small. The main source of new jobs was the expansion of existing establishments, which provided a 14.9 per cent increase in employment, or about six out of every ten job gains. Moves into the region from outside provided a

Table 5.3 *Shift-share analysis of manufacturing employment change by type of area: East Midlands 1968–75*

	Manufacturing employment in 1968 thousands	as % 1968 employment			
		National component	Structural component	Differential shift	Actual change
Cities	285.0	−10.0	−2.0	+ 3.9	− 8.1
Larger towns	77.4	−10.0	+1.9	+ 6.6	− 1.5
Smaller towns	161.8	−10.0	−3.6	+18.6	+ 5.0
Rural areas	43.5	−10.0	+1.8	+25.0	+16.8
East Midlands	567.6	−10.0	−0.1	+ 8.6	− 1.5

1968 base year, MLH disaggregation.
See Appendix B for definition of areas.

Table 5.4 The components of manufacturing employment change by type of area: East Midlands 1968–75

| | Openings | | | Survivors[1] | | Closures | Transfers[2] out | Net change |
| | as % 1968 manufacturing employment in each area | | | | | | | |
	New firms	Local branches[3]	Moves in[4]	Expansions	Contractions			
Cities	+3.6	+3.5	+0.9	+11.9	−15.6	−12.2	−0.2	− 8.1
Larger towns	+2.9	+4.1	+4.1	+11.5	−13.7	−10.3	0	− 1.5
Smaller towns	+4.8	+3.4	+4.0	+18.5	−12.4	−13.2	−0.1	+ 5.0
Rural areas	+6.2	+2.9	+5.3	+24.9	−12.7	− 9.4	−0.4	+16.8
East Midlands	+4.1	+3.5	+2.2	+14.9	−14.3	−12.0	0	− 1.5

[1]includes transfers internal to each type of area.
[2]transfers out to another type of area in the East Midlands.
[3]branches and subsidiaries opened by firms operating in the region in 1968.
[4]transfers in, plus new branches and subsidiaries of firms not operating in the region in 1968.

2.2 per cent increase, and new branches and subsidiaries set up by existing local firms another 3.5 per cent. The remaining increase in employment—4.1 per cent, or 23,000 jobs—was provided by entirely new independent firms, a contribution which mainly reflects the large number of new firms set up during the period—no less than 1,650—rather than their average size, which was only 14 employees in 1975. The large gross gains and losses found in the region as a whole are also found in each of the four types of area within the region, but the most important aspect of Table 5.4 concerns the differences between these areas.

Urban-rural differences

Roughly two-thirds of the overall disparity in growth between cities and rural areas is due to employment change in surviving plants, that is, plants operating at both the beginning and the end of the period. In particular it is the *expansion* of these plants, rather than the location of contraction, which differentiates cities from small towns and rural areas. The location of expansion in surviving plants accounts for a little over half the total difference in employment change between cities and rural areas.

The location of moves into the region disadvantages the cities relative to other areas, mirroring the pattern which we have already identified across the country as a whole. On the other hand, complete transfers out of the cities to elsewhere in the region are relatively unimportant: between 1968 and 1975 they accounted for only a 0.2 per cent decline in the cities' employment, or roughly 600 jobs. There is also no evidence that new branches and subsidiaries set up by local companies are creating more jobs in smaller towns and rural areas than in the cities.

New firms provide more jobs in small towns and rural areas than in cities, though their contribution is modest everywhere: firms founded between 1968 and 1975 accounted for only about one-tenth of the overall urban-rural shift in the East Midlands over that same period. However, this conclusion is to some extent misleading. As we show in the next chapter, the main contrast in the location of new firms is between towns dominated by large manufacturing plants, where rates of new-firm formation are particularly low, and the rest. Though there is evidence of an urban-rural contrast in new-firm formation this is much less marked.

Probably the most surprising aspect of Table 5.4 is how little the loss of jobs through closures varies between urban and rural areas. It is certainly true that closures have been substantial in the cities—accounting for the disappearance of one in eight of their

Table 5.5   The growth of manufacturing plants by size: East Midlands 1968–75

Size in 1968 (employees)	as % 1968 employment in each size band		
	Change in survivors	Closures	Net change
1–25	+46.2	−33.5	+12.7
26–100	+19.8	−23.0	− 3.2
101–500	+ 0.4	−15.3	−14.9
501+	−11.5	− 3.2	−14.7
All plants	+ 0.7	−12.0	−11.3

manufacturing jobs between 1968 and 1975—but they have been scarcely less important elsewhere. Indeed, the difference in closure rates is equal to less than one-quarter of the urban-rural disparity in the expansion of surviving establishments.

At this stage however, any conclusion about variations in rates of growth and closure must remain tentative because the differences between urban and rural areas may result from the structural characteristics of the plants in each area. One such structural characteristic, the mix of industries, cannot explain urban-rural contrasts in the East Midlands, as we demonstrated earlier, but the size of manufacturing plants in each area is rather more important. Table 5.5 shows that very small manufacturing plants have provided a net increase in employment while larger plants have declined. Small plants are also more likely to close, but if they survive they are more likely to grow quickly. The influence of size on growth is pervasive, and swamps any differences that are due to corporate status (Fothergill and Gudgin 1979c). For example, small establishments are more likely to close than large ones—and more likely to show healthy growth if they remain open—whether they are independent firms, branch plants or subsidiary companies. The implication is that an area with a high proportion of small plants can expect to experience both above-average closure rates and above-average expansion among surviving firms.

Table 5.6 shows rates of expansion, contraction and closure, after having standardised for differences in plant size. What we have done here is to compare the actual rates, in each of the four types of area, with a predicted rate based upon the size structure of plants in each area, and average rates of expansion, contraction and closure in each size-band in the region as a whole. What emerges is that the urban-rural contrasts identified earlier, in Table 5.4, are not spurious. Even after standardising for size, the rates of expansion, contraction and closure are all worse in the cities, and the expansion

Table 5.6   Rates of manufacturing employment change by type of area: East Midlands 1968–75 (standardised for differences in plant size)

| | Predicted[1] = 100 | | |
	Expansion	Contraction	Closure
Cities	82	109	105
Larger towns	91	91	105
Smaller towns	119	90	99
Rural areas	151	93	69

[1] on the basis of rates in eight size bands in the region as a whole and the employment in each size band in each area in 1968.

of surviving establishments continues to show much the largest urban-rural contrast. So neither industrial structure nor size structure explains away urban-rural differences. To check this conclusion we have also standardised for industry and size *simultaneously*, but this too makes little noticeable difference. It appears that there is some aspect of larger settlements which leads to higher closures, higher losses through contractions, and above all to a much lower rate of expansion in surviving firms.

One possibility is that the firms in cities are hiving-off growth into new branch plants because they cannot expand their existing factories, whereas firms in smaller towns and rural areas, less hemmed in by existing urban development, are able to expand on-site. To test this hypothesis we attached an 'origin' to each of the new branches and subsidiaries set up in the region by East Midlands firms. In addition the Department of Industry kindly provided figures for the employment in new branches set up outside the region. Table 5.7 shows the results. Firms in the cities certainly generate rather more jobs in new local branches, both in the cities and elsewhere, than their counterparts in rural areas, but they are no more likely to set up new branches outside the region. This suggests that city-based firms which are contemplating local expansion are more likely to be forced into setting up branches nearby instead of keeping their growth on-site. However, the important point is that if all these new branch plants are bundled together with their parent plants then city-based firms are still not generating as many jobs as other firms. Indeed, urban-rural disparities in growth hardly narrow at all. The problem with cities is not simply that their firms are diverting growth to other areas, but rather that city-based firms are growing more slowly than their rivals elsewhere.

Table 5.7   The diversion of expansion into new branches: East Midlands 1968–75

| | | as % 1968 manufacturing employment in each area | | | |
| | Change in existing plants[1] | Employment created in new branches[2] | | | Total job generation by existing firms |
		In same area	Elsewhere in region	Outside region[3]	
Cities	−15.9	+3.1	+1.3	+2.2	−9.3
Larger towns	−12.5	+2.6	+0.1	+1.8	−8.0
Smaller towns	−7.2	+1.6	+1.0	+2.9	−1.7
Rural areas	+2.8	+1.6	+0.8	+2.1	+7.3

[1] net change in survivors less closures.
[2] new branches and subsidiaries opened after 1968 by firms which operated in the region in 1968.
[3] Department of Industry estimates 1966–75.

Table 5.8 Manufacturing employment change in single and multi-plant firms by type of area: East Midlands 1968–75

| | Employment change[1] in existing factories as % of 1968 employment in each type of each area | |
	Single plant independent firms	Multi-plant firms
Cities	−9.5	−17.8
Larger towns	−5.1	−13.6
Smaller towns	−3.8	−7.9
Rural areas	+2.7	+2.9
East Midlands	−6.8	−12.6

[1]net change in survivors less closures.

It might still be the case that the expansion generated by plants in cities is being diverted into *existing* branches in smaller towns and rural areas. This is of course possible only in firms which operate more than one factory. Consequently, if it is occurring on a large scale it should not be difficult to identify because the factories belonging to multi-plant companies will show much greater urban-rural contrasts in growth than single plant firms. Table 5.8 shows that the factories operated by multi-plant firms *do* display larger urban-rural contrasts in employment change, which suggests that some diversion of production and jobs from the cities into existing factories elsewhere is probably occurring. But the notable feature of the table is the strong and consistent urban-rural contrast in growth which also characterises single plant independent firms. The marked contrast in growth among these single plant firms provides further telling evidence that the problem in cities is not simply that firms are moving out, but also that the firms which remain face severe locational handicaps which undermine their growth.

So far we have looked only at the period from 1968 to 1975, though our earlier evidence showed that the urban-rural shift in manufacturing employment started well before the late 1960s. This is important because it raises the possibility that the components of change over a comparatively short period may be an imperfect guide to long-run differences between cities and small towns. However, for one part of the East Midlands, Leicestershire, the data allows us to examine rates of opening, growth and closure over the much longer period stretching back to 1947. As elsewhere in the region and in the

Table 5.9   The components of manufacturing employment change: Leicestershire 1947–75

	Base year employment thousands	as % base year manufacturing employment in each period					
		New firms[1]	New branches[2]	Net change[3] in survivors	Closures	Net transfers	Net change
Greater Leicester[4]							
1947–56	91.0	+ 4.8	+ 4.7	+11.2	– 8.4	–0.1	+12.3
1956–68	102.1	+ 5.0	+ 5.7	+10.2	–20.3	–0.8	– 0.2
1968–75	102.3	+ 6.1	+ 4.9	– 0.9	–15.9	–0.2	– 6.0
1947–75	91.0	+20.2	+14.6	+12.4	–40.8	–0.6	+ 5.7
Rest of Leicestershire							
1947–56	54.3	+ 3.2	+ 6.0	+ 8.2	– 8.9	+0.2	+ 8.6
1956–68	59.0	+ 6.1	+ 8.0	+11.3	–17.0	+1.4	+ 9.9
1968–75	64.8	+ 4.9	+ 5.7	+ 6.2	–14.1	+0.2	+ 2.9
1947–75	54.3	+17.0	+23.9	+14.8	–33.3	+0.3	+22.8

[1] includes branches of new firms.
[2] includes moves in from outside Leicestershire.
[3] includes transfers within each area.
[4] defined as Leicester, Oadby and Wigston, and Blaby districts.
N.B. The components of change compare plants present at the beginning and end of any period (e.g. 1947 and 1975 or 1968 and 1975). Therefore the changes in individual periods do not sum to changes in the period as a whole because some plants both open and close during the full 1947–75 period.

rest of Britain, manufacturing employment has grown more slowly in Leicester itself, the main urban centre, than in its rural and small town hinterland.

On the whole the figures for Leicestershire since 1947, in Table 5.9, confirm the conclusions drawn from the shorter 1968–75 period. The complete transfer of firms out of Leicester city into its hinterland has little to do with the disparity in employment change, and the location of new firms cannot explain urban-rural shifts in the county either. Indeed, new independent firms have actually provided more jobs in Leicester city itself. In other respects the figures for 1947–75 differ slightly from those already observed. The greater employment in new branch plants in small town and rural Leicestershire accounts for about half the area's better growth over the full period—which makes new branches a more important source of urban-rural differences than we found during shorter periods. The higher loss of jobs in closures in Leicester city also makes an important contribution to the urban-rural shift within the county, whereas the earlier evidence suggested that closure rates do not vary greatly between cities and small towns. But, in part, these differences between the long-term and short-term components of change reflect factors specific to Leicestershire. In particular, the higher proportion of employment in small firms in Leicester city tends to boost the loss of jobs in closures and improve growth among surviving firms, given the higher rates of closure and growth which characterise small firms. Our earlier conclusions concerning the components of change therefore need not be modified very much by this long view of rural growth and urban decline.

A more important feature of Table 5.9 is the difference between time periods. After 1968 Leicestershire exhibits the familiar pattern of a large urban-rural contrast in the growth of surviving establishments, with little difference in the loss of jobs in closures; before 1968 this pattern was much less in evidence. In the early post-war years up to 1956 the city actually experienced a better rate of employment growth than its hinterland, mainly due to greater expansion among its surviving firms. In subsequent years Leicestershire—in common with the rest of Britain—began to display urban-rural contrasts in growth, though the strong contrast in the growth of surviving plants, which we showed is such an important part of urban-rural shifts in the East Midlands as a whole, did not emerge until after 1968.

The Components of Change: Evidence from Elsewhere
The East Midlands data provide a detailed picture of how the opening, growth and closure of firms contributes to the urban-rural

shift, but unfortunately this region lacks a major conurbation where the decline in manufacturing has been more acute. What we now need to do therefore is to compare the East Midlands figures with those from conurbations. Firstly we examine Manchester, for which good data is available, and secondly we look at London, for which the data is not so good, but which is particularly interesting because its size and rate of manufacturing decline make it unique in Britain. Finally, these British examples are compared with evidence of the urban-rural shift in the United States.

Manchester

The establishment-based data for Manchester, assembled by Lloyd and Dicken, is broadly similar to that for the East Midlands—both data sets are based upon the records of the Factory Inspectorate—which facilitates comparisons. But the loss of manufacturing jobs in Manchester, as in other conurbations, has been much more acute than in the free standing cities of the East Midlands. The Manchester data shows that between 1966 and 1975 manufacturing employment fell by 25 per cent, compared with a fall of only 8 per cent in the cities of the East Midlands between 1968 and 1975. The components of change in Manchester, shown in Table 5.10, support some of the conclusions which emerged from the East Midlands data. The contribution of new independent firms is slightly below average in the cities of the East Midlands, and new firms are still less important in the Manchester conurbation, which suggests that the location of new firms probably plays a small part in the overall urban-rural shift in industrial location. The contribution of new branch plants to employment growth is also lower in Manchester, again confirming the trend within the East Midlands.

Other aspects of the figures for Manchester are surprising. The urban-rural shift within the East Midlands primarily reflects differences in the rate of growth of surviving establishments, rather than the loss of jobs in closures, but the greater decline in Manchester reflects a much larger loss of jobs in closures, while the growth of surviving establishments appears to be only marginally worse than in the cities of the East Midlands. Nevertheless, these superficial contrasts are misleading for three reasons. Firstly, as a result of its dependence on the declining textile industry Manchester has a particularly unfavourable industrial structure which can be expected to exacerbate the loss of jobs through closures. We estimate that this adverse industrial structure led to a five per cent fall in Manchester's manufacturing employment, relative to the country as

Table 5.10 *The components of manufacturing employment change in Manchester and the East Midlands*

	as % base year manufacturing employment				
	New firms	New branches and moves in	Net change in survivors[1]	Closures	Net change
Manchester conurbation 1966–75	+2.8	+4.0	−6.3	−25.4	−24.9
East Midlands: cities 1968–75	+3.6	+4.4	−3.9	−12.2	− 8.1
East Midlands: rest 1968–75	+4.6	+7.8	+4.5	−11.8	+ 5.1

[1]includes local transfers.
Source: Manchester from Lloyd and Dicken (1979)

a whole, between 1966 and 1975 (Fothergill and Gudgin 1979a). Secondly, the figures for Manchester relate to a longer period than those for the East Midlands. And thirdly, Manchester has a higher proportion of its employment in small establishments, which, as we demonstrated earlier, tends to boost both the numbers of jobs lost in closures and the average growth among surviving firms.

It is possible to adjust for the last two of these factors by calculating 'predicted' employment changes in closures and surviving establishments, based on the size of plants in Manchester and the average annual rates of growth and closure in each size band in the East Midlands. The difference between the actual and predicted employment change in Manchester is the correct measure of the extent to which rates of growth and closure are worse than those found in the East Midlands. Table 5.11 shows that though Manchester's loss of jobs in closures is higher than expected, the main reason for its greater decline is the much poorer growth among surviving establishments—over ten per cent worse than predicted on the basis of trends in the East Midlands. In other words, despite superficial contrasts the components of employment change in Manchester, a conurbation, are very much in line with what we would expect on the basis of urban-rural contrasts in the East Midlands.

At this stage we should issue a word of caution: despite what has been said so far, not all areas experience rates of opening, closure and growth which fit so neatly into the urban-rural continuum we have identified. Lloyd and Dicken have stressed the difference between Manchester and Merseyside, the other conurbation for which they hold data. Indeed, between 1966 and 1975 Merseyside experienced no net loss of manufacturing jobs. The differences between Manchester and Merseyside are partly due to Merseyside

Table 5.11 Actual and predicted manufacturing employment change in Manchester 1966–75

	as % 1966 manufacturing employment	
	Net change in survivors	Closures
Actual	−6.3	−25.4
Predicted[1]	+5.0	−19.8
Difference	−11.3	− 5.6

[1] on the basis of average annual rates of growth and closure in eight size bands in the East Midlands 1968–75, and the employment in each size band in Manchester in 1966.

being dominated by very large manufacturing plants—two-thirds of its employment is in plants with 500 workers or more—and as we have seen, large plants are less likely to close, but are more likely to experience contraction than expansion. Another reason for the differences is that Merseyside, unlike Manchester or the East Midlands, has been designated a special development area. This has led to a much higher level of in-movement of new branch plants, attracted by grants and subsidies. It has also led to a better rate of expansion among existing plants (at least up to 1975) due to the continuing growth to mature employment levels of some of the big branch plants, particularly in the motor industry, which moved into Merseyside in the early 1960s.

London
If Manchester's manufacturing decline has been steep then London's has been precipitous. Between 1959 and 1975 the capital lost 38 per cent of its manufacturing employment, or nearly 600,000 jobs, much more than anywhere else in Britain. Unfortunately, suitable establishment-based data is not available for London, so that a detailed comparison is impossible. However, it is commonly believed that London has suffered from an exceptionally high rate of closure of manufacturing plants. This belief has its origins in a study by Dennis (1978) who used the Department of Industry's records to examine employment decline in Greater London between 1966 and 1974. He found that 14 per cent of London's manufacturing jobs—equal to nearly half the total net loss—disappeared in complete closures unassociated with movement.

Table 5.12   The components of manufacturing employment change in London and the East Midlands

	as % base year employment			
	Net movement[1]	Closures[2]	Residual	*Net change*
London 1966–74	−8.0	−14.2	− 8.0	−30.2
East Midlands: cities 1968–75	−2.6	−10.4	+ 4.9	− 8.1
East Midlands: rest 1968–75	+0.7	−10.2	+14.6	+ 5.1

[1] transfers and new branches, including inter-regional moves.
[2] complete closures unassociated with movement in plants employing 20+.
Source: London from Dennis (1978).

Table 5.12 compares London and the East Midlands. To maintain comparability the figures for closures in the East Midlands exclude plants employing fewer than twenty people, which were excluded from Dennis's data, but the periods covered differ slightly. The comparison shows that, in fact, closures have been only slightly more important in London than in the East Midlands. What is more, even this difference may only reflect the smaller average size of manufacturing plants in London, which will tend to boost the loss of jobs through closures. In Table 5.12 the largest part of the contrast with the East Midlands is accounted for by the 'residual', which includes employment change in surviving plants and in new firms and new branch plants. As new firms and new branches make only modest contributions to employment growth, the residual therefore suggests that London's job losses relative to everywhere else probably reflect a much more adverse balance between expansion and contraction in surviving plants. In other words the problem in London concerns the growth of its firms, not the likelihood of their closure. In this respect, of course, London's decline is no different to the decline of the cities in the East Midlands.

The United States

We are now beginning to assemble a reliable picture of the way in which the urban-rural shift is being brought about, though at this stage we have still said nothing about the underlying causes. It seems that in Britain the shift to small towns is mainly the result of the location of growth, particularly the growth in existing plants, rather than the location of decline, which is much more uniformly spread. However, since the urban-rural shift is a widespread phenomenon which characterises most Western industrial countries it is worth looking briefly at the evidence from one of these, the United States, to see how far the British experience can be generalised to elsewhere.

Allaman and Birch (1975) have examined the components of change in metropolitan and rural areas in the United States, using data originally collected by a credit-rating company, Dun and Bradstreet Ltd. In certain important details this data is not comparable with British figures, and covers only a very short time period, but it can be used to provide a meaningful contrast within the United States (Table 5.13). As in Britain, transfers—complete 'lock, stock and barrel' relocations—are unimportant in differentiating metropolitan and rural areas, and the opening of new plants (branches and new firms) favours rural areas but only

Table 5.13 *The components of manufacturing employment change in the United States 1970–2*

as % 1970 manufacturing employment

| | Openings | Survivors | | Closures | Transfers | | Net change |
		Expansions	Contractions		In	Out	
Metropolitan areas	+3.0	+ 9.1	−10.2	−11.8	+0.2	−0.2	−10.0
Rural areas	+3.5	+11.3	− 8.1	−12.3	+0.4	−0.2	− 5.5

Source: Allaman and Birch (1975).

accounts for a small part of the difference. Closures, too, cannot explain the decline of the metropolitan areas, and actually account for rather more jobs in rural areas, something we did not encounter in Britain. Once again, therefore, it is the growth of existing manufacturing establishments—the balance between expansions and contractions—which has been the mechanism through which the urban-rural shift has been brought about in the United States. In other words, the British and American experiences seem very similar.

Urban Decline and Rural Growth in Different Kinds of Firm
So far this chapter has looked at the way in which the urban-rural shift in manufacturing has been brought about. Now we will look at the kinds of firm that are declining in cities and growing elsewhere. This information is particularly useful in the last part of the chapter when we set out an explanation for the urban-rural shift. The analysis of growth in different sorts of firm must however be restricted to the East Midlands because of the lack of suitable data for other areas.

Let us start with the role of corporate status. In some academic literature on urban and regional growth certain groups of firms are often cast in a much worse light than others. Typically, it is the externally owned and controlled companies, particularly the multi-nationals, which receive all the criticism. They allegedly move their capital around the country (and the world) in the pursuit of private profit, with scant regard for the communities they exploit and then leave derelict. This group of companies, run from London or Detroit, is sometimes accused of single-handedly engineering the downfall first of the depressed regions and more recently the inner city. There can be little doubt that these firms do indeed move their capital from place to place as it suits them. However, it has never been proved that their locational behaviour is really any different from the rest of the population of firms.

In Table 5.14 we have therefore divided up the manufacturing plants in the East Midlands according to different aspects of their corporate status, and compared employment change in each of these broad categories in the cities and the rest of the region. The first point to note is that the overall level of employment change varies with corporate status. In the region as a whole, locally owned firms have experienced much better employment growth than non-locally owned firms. Mostly this reflects differences in plant size, as locally owned firms are smaller on average, and small plants tend to grow faster than larger ones. Another notable difference in employment

Table 5.14 *Manufacturing employment change by corporate status and type of area: East Midlands 1968–75*

as % 1968 employment in each type in each area

	Control		Ownership		Ranking		Take-over	
	Local[1]	non-local	Local[1]	non-local	Top 100 U.K. firms	Others	Acquired 1968–75	non-acquired
Cities	−8.2	−7.5	− 2.9	−12.8	−9.6	−7.5	−26.5	−6.5
Rest of region	+5.4	+3.8	+16.2	− 4.0	−3.3	+7.6	−23.4	+7.7
East Midlands	−1.8	−0.7	+ 5.6	− 8.1	−6.6	+0.1	−24.9	+0.5

[1] local = same sub-region.

change is that between firms taken over between 1968 and 1975, who lost a quarter of their employment, and non-acquired firms, whose growth was markedly better.

The main point in Table 5.14, however, is that urban-rural differences in employment change are evident in each category of firms. Thus locally owned firms are on balance a better bet for employment growth, but they show much slower growth in cities than elsewhere, as do non-local firms. The only exceptions are acquired companies, which seem to decline equally rapidly everywhere. This conclusion—that regardless of corporate status, manufacturing firms grow more slowly in cities—is of some importance because it demonstrates that the blame for the decline of the cities cannot be pinned on any one type of firm. The giant multi-national corporation is no more to blame than the locally-owned enterprise. The locational handicaps experienced in cities affect a wide range of firms, regardless of who owns and controls them.

Another popular belief about the decline of the cities is that the problem is caused by a disproportionately large share of 'old' manufacturing firms. It is never quite clear in this context whether 'old' is supposed to refer to the industries found in cities, for instance textiles rather than electronics, or whether it refers to the age of the firms themselves. We have already shown that over the

Table 5.15   Manufacturing employment change by age of establishment: Leicestershire 1968–75

	% of 1968 employment	% change 1968–75
Greater Leicester		
Firms new 1947–68	9.4	+29.2
Branches[1] new 1947–68	9.2	−14.8
Pre-1947 plants	81.4	−22.4
All plants operating in 1968	100.0	−16.9
Rest of Leicestershire		
Firms new 1947–68	7.9	+21.1
Branches[1] new 1947–68	13.8	+ 5.4
Pre-1947 plants	78.3	−13.1
All plants operating in 1968	100.0	− 7.8

[1] includes subsidiaries.

Table 5.16 Employment change[1] in existing manufacturing plants by size and type of area: East Midlands 1968–75

	as % of 1968 employment in each size band in each area			
	Plant size in 1968			
	1–25	*26–100*	*101–500*	*501+*
Cities	+11.6	−10.6	−19.5	−17.8
Larger towns	− 2.2	+ 1.3	−15.1	−14.9
Smaller towns	+19.2	+ 3.3	−14.7	− 8.0
Rural areas	+ 3.2	+ 6.2	+ 7.9	− 3.5
East Midlands	+12.7	− 3.2	−14.9	−14.7

[1] net change in survivors less closures.

country as a whole, industrial structure (the mix of old declining and new growing industries) cannot explain the decline of the cities, so that possibility can be dismissed. On the question of the age of firms, some light can be shed by examining the establishment records for Leicestershire.

Table 5.15 compares Leicester with its small town and rural hinterland, where manufacturing employment growth has been markedly quicker since the mid-1950s. The two areas differ little in their mix of old and new establishments. Even in 1968 roughly four-fifths of all the manufacturing jobs in both areas were in plants which opened before 1947, and Leicester itself actually had a slightly higher proportion of its jobs in new firms. The difference between the two areas has in fact been due to slower growth in the city among both pre-1947 establishments and new branch plants, though, interestingly, new firms grew slightly more quickly in the city. At least in Leicestershire the age of firms does not offer a satisfactory explanation for urban-rural disparities in employment change.

Neither corporate status nor the age of firms therefore take us very far towards a better understanding of which firms are bringing about urban-rural shifts. So far, it appears that slower growth in the cities characterises a wide range of firms. However, when we look closer two important contrasts emerge.

The first concerns plant size. Table 5.16 shows employment change by size between 1968 and 1975 in all the establishments which were operating in the East Midlands in 1968. The faster growth of small plants is something we have noted before, so this need not detain us, but the important finding in the table is that

Table 5.17   Employment change[1] in existing manufacturing plants in industries with high and low rates of investment: East Midlands 1968–75

	as % 1968 employment in each group in each area	
	High investment industries[2]	Low investment industries
Cities	−16.9	−15.1
Larger towns	−12.9	−12.2
Smaller towns	+ 1.1	−14.6
Rural areas	+17.5	−12.8
East Midlands	− 7.9	−14.4

[1] net change in survivors less closures.
[2] rate of investment greater than 75 per cent of average U.K. manufacturing investment per employee.

there is no evidence for systematic urban-rural contrasts in growth among the very smallest establishments, employing 25 people or less. Quite what this means is not clear. On the one hand there has been much speculative discussion about how cities, and the inner city in particular, provide a good environment for small manufacturing units. Our evidence does not prove this point, but it certainly does not contradict it. On the other hand the relative buoyancy of very small firms in the cities may not be so much the result of the environment which cities provide as a reflection of the characteristics of very small firms themselves, wherever they are located. They usually operate in run-down premises, use non-union labour, and rely heavily on personal contacts to secure orders. Success or failure depends a great deal on the skills and judgement of the manager. When compared to the influence of individual entrepreneurial ability, more systematic influences associated with location may not be very important in determining the fate of small firms.

The second contrast which can be identified among the population of firms is between industries with high and low rates of investment. In Table 5.17 industries have been grouped into two broad categories according to the rate of investment per employee shown by Census of Production data for 1968, 1970 and 1972 for each industry (MLH) in the country as a whole. The difference between the two categories is striking. Urban-rural contrasts in the growth of manufacturing plants are entirely concentrated in industries with high rates of investment. There is no evidence that plants in industries with low rates of investment experience systematic urban-rural contrasts in growth.

This is an important conclusion, and one which needs to be checked.

Chapter 4 noted that inter-regional shifts in employment are concentrated in industries which are expanding their employment. One possibility is that a large urban-rural contrast in industries with high rates of investment occurs simply because these industries are also the ones which are expanding their employment. In fact this is not the case. The industries with high rates of investment and below average growth of employment show sharp urban-rural contrasts in employment change, but there is little evidence of urban-rural shifts in industries with low rates of investment and above average growth of employment. In other words, the main influence upon the rate at which an industry shifts its employment to smaller towns and rural areas is its rate of investment, not its employment change. Any explanation for the urban-rural shift must therefore identify not only an underlying cause which differentiates cities from small towns, but also one which at the same time can differentiate between industries with high and low rates of investment.

Urban-Rural Differences in Profitability
We have now accumulated a great deal of evidence on the ways in which the urban-rural shift is occurring, and about the sorts of firms which are responsible for the shift. Before we move on to consider the underlying causes it is useful to investigate one final aspect of the urban-rural contrast in manufacturing: differences in profitability. For this, we selected a sample of companies in two industries, mechanical engineering and clothing. The data is described in Appendix A. It covers firms from all regions of Great Britain but excludes those firms which have substantial operations in more than one of our six types of area. The definition of profitability that has

Table 5.18 Average profitability[1] by type of area 1971–5

	Mechanical engineering		Clothing	
	No. of firms	Profitability U.K. = 100	No. of firms	Profitability U.K. = 100
London	35	105	43	87
Conurbations	67	86	64	88
Free standing cities	55	96	30	106
Industrial towns	32	103	15	110
County towns and rural areas	45	122	28	134

[1] post-tax return on capital employed, standardised for industry differences.

been used is the post-tax return on capital employed, adjusted to allow for varying levels of profitability in individual industries within the broad categories of mechanical engineering and clothing.

The results, Table 5.18, show that in both these contrasting industries profitability is higher in small towns and rural areas than in cities. Only mechanical engineering in London disturbs the progression of declining profits with increasing urbanisation. The firms included in this table are mainly medium sized, because the largest firms in each industry tend to operate several plants in a range of different types of area, but the evidence nevertheless points clearly to disadvantages which are strong enough to squeeze the profits of firms in urban locations. Research by the Centre for Interfirm Comparison (1977), using data on a smaller sample of companies in a wider range of industries, confirms this conclusion and also suggests that profits very more between cities and small towns than between regions.

Alternative Explanations of the Urban-Rural Shift

The aim so far in this chapter has been to describe the main characteristics of the diversion of manufacturing jobs out of cities and into small towns and rural areas. As this evidence forms the basis for an explanation of the urban-rural shift it is worth summarising.

1. The association between settlement size and manufacturing employment change is remarkably close. The larger a town, the faster on average its decline.
2. The shift from urban to rural areas is found in the other Western industrial countries for which we have information, even where the national economic context is very different to that in Britain.
3. In Britain, at least, the shift proceeded more rapidly in the 1960s and 1970s than in the 1950s.
4. The location of growth—in existing factories and to a lesser extent in new factories—is more important than the location of decline (contractions and closures) in bringing about the urban-rural shift.
5. The poorer growth in cities characterises a wide range of establishments, irrespective of their corporate status.
6. Very small manufacturing establishments do not however fare any worse in cities, unlike larger establishments.
7. The better growth outside the cities is concentrated in industries with high rates of investment.
8. Company profitability appears to be lower in cities.

Any complete explanation for the urban-rural shift should be able to account for all the above characteristics and, even better, should allow an accurate prediction of the strength of the shift which has occurred. Any explanation which by itself accounts for only one or two of these characteristics must be viewed as weak, though it is possible of course that the urban-rural shift is the result of a combination of factors, each accounting for a few characteristics, which collectively offer a satisfactory explanation.

A number of potential explanations have been advanced in academic literature, chiefly in the context of inner city decline. These include the idea that cities have an inferior mix of industries, shortages of labour, old-fashioned premises, and unattractive residential environments, with planning controls acting as an additional hindrance. In general these explanations have not been convincing because they have been based on very limited empirical information about the nature of the urban-rural shift and the mechanisms through which these underlying causes are supposed to lead to disparities in growth. The evidence we have presented has already dismissed two such hypotheses. Industrial structure—the mix of industries in cities—explains none of the urban-rural shift, and if we can generalise from the figures for one county, the age of manufacturing establishments also has little to do with urban decline. Furthermore, we have shown that the blame for decline in the cities cannot be pinned on any one group of firms, such as large multi-national companies.

It is our contention that the single overriding cause of the urban-rural shift in industrial location is the lack of space for physical expansion faced by a large proportion of factories in urban areas. Although other disadvantages may exacerbate the relative decline of the cities, the constraining role of a continuous built-up area is sufficient by itself to account for all eight of the characteristics of the urban-rural shift listed above. This also satisfactorily explains the magnitude of the employment changes which have occurred in urban and rural areas in recent years. But before outlining the reasoning behind this conclusion we should briefly say why some of the alternative arguments are inadequate.

Labour problems

Labour is such an important element in all industrial activity that it figures in most theories of growth concerning regions or cities and small towns, and direct approaches to firms invariably reveal labour difficulties of some description. A major survey of industrial moves for example (Department of Trade and Industry 1973) found that inadequate premises and unsatisfactory labour supply were the main reasons why expanding firms chose to open new plants in new locations. The role of labour in the urban-rural shift therefore needs to be examined closely. In fact there are three separate aspects of labour supply which might in theory generate disparities in growth. These are availability, cost and militancy.

In a period of relatively full employment the availability of labour is likely to be a pervasive influence on the location of expansion, but even in the 1950s and 1960s, when rates of unemployment were much lower, the pattern of labour availability was never one which presented shortages in cities and surpluses in small towns. Indeed, three of the declining conurbations—Clydeside, Tyneside and Merseyside—have experienced persistently above-average rates of unemployment, while some of the fast-growing county towns and rural areas of southern England have had continuously low unemployment. The supply of labour becoming available in small towns through the decline of agriculture and mining, and through increases in female activity rates (which were initially quite low in these places), has also never been sufficient to match manufacturing industry's growing demand for labour outside the cities. The expansion of the supply of labour in small towns has therefore been met largely by in-migration but, except for one or two unusual cases, such as Cornwall, migration has not occurred in advance of job creation to the extent that a large pool of unemployed labour has developed. Rather than jobs following people into small towns and rural areas, it seems much more likely that migration has occurred in response to rising employment, as a factor permitting growth outside major cities.

In several important respects labour availability also fails to explain the characteristics of the urban-rural shift. In particular, if labour availability was the major factor causing the urban-rural shift it is most unlikely that the shift would have accelerated after 1960, because the labour shortages facing British industry have eased rather than intensified since the 1950s as unemployment has risen everywhere. In any case, there is no reason why labour shortages should cause the association between growth and settlement size to be so close, or explain why the better growth outside the cities is concentrated in industries with high rates of investment. It remains possible that in some cases, and at some times, labour shortages in urban areas have given rise to a shift of employment to small towns and rural areas, but there is no case for believing this to be an important general explanation for the urban-rural shift.

Much the same conclusion applies to the cost of labour. Moore,

Table 5.19 *The incidence of strikes in the conurbations 1968–73*

	Days lost in local stoppages per thousand employees (U.K. = 100)	
	Actual	Standardised for mix of industries
London	31	38
Birmingham	168	67
Manchester	92	93
West Yorkshire	37	28
Clydeside	257	227
Merseyside	364	261
Tyneside	205	105

Source: Smith *et al.* (1978).

Rhodes and Tyler (1980) examined manufacturing wages and salaries per employee in the conurbations and their hinterlands and did not find a consistent pattern. In some conurbations earnings are higher than the national average and in others lower, and the same is true of hinterland areas. For example London, which has experienced the most rapid manufacturing decline, has the highest level of earnings of any of the conurbations, but the rest of the South East, which has experienced healthy growth, has equally high earnings. Furthermore, the divergences from national earnings levels are rarely more than a few percentage points.

A major study of strikes (Smith *et al.* 1978) illustrates the absence of a consistent record of labour militancy in Britain's largest cities. Table 5.19 shows the days lost in 'local' stoppages in each of the conurbations. Because some industries are strike-prone wherever they are located, this table also shows the strike rates after adjusting for the mix of industries in each conurbation. What is noticeable is the contrast among these areas. In Merseyside and Clydeside the strike rate is substantially above the national average, and in West Yorkshire and London it is well below, yet all these conurbations have lost manufacturing jobs more quickly than elsewhere. The complexity of the pattern of strike activity extends beyond the conurbations: among free standing cities and industrial towns, some are well above the national average and others far below. This evidence makes it extremely difficult to explain the urban-rural shift in terms of labour militancy.

Residential preference
An alternative idea which must also be rejected as a major explanation for the urban-rural shift is that manufacturing employ-

ment is growing in small towns and rural areas because these are the places in which people now want to live. Keeble found an association between manufacturing employment growth and residentially attractive areas in his study of U.K. employment change between 1966 and 1971 (Keeble 1976) and argued that residential preference played a major role in determining the pattern of industrial location. However, his more recent investigation of employment change between 1971 and 1976 failed to identify the same association (Keeble 1980). This explanation is weak not only because its relevance seems to vary over time, but also because it relies on simple geographical association, rather than an analysis of the mechanisms through which residential preference effects growth, and it fails to account for many of the observed characteristics of the urban-rural shift. While it is true that environmentally attractive rural and coastal areas have gained a growing share of U.K. industry, this has not necessarily occurred because they are attractive. As evidence for this, witness the healthy growth of manufacturing outside the cities in environmentally unattractive places, such as the coalfield areas of Yorkshire, Derbyshire and Nottinghamshire, as well as in more obviously desirable locations.

More importantly, explanations which rely on residential preference are most relevant to the location of *new* factories, when an element of real choice faces managers. Yet as we have noted, urban-rural differences in growth primarily reflect disparities in the growth of *existing* factories. Residential preference cannot explain why, given two apparently similar existing manufacturing plants, one located in a city and one in a small town, the plant in the small town will usually show better employment growth, even if the two plants are independent single-site firms. The most likely explanation for the employment growth in many attractive areas away from Britain's cities is not that they are attractive, but that they have room for industrial expansion, in common with unattractive areas, such as coalfields, which have fared equally well. Similarly, industry in most seaside resorts is predominantly in peripheral locations with room for further expansion. Residential preference may be advantageous, but is probably largely coincidental in the urban-rural shift.

Planning policies
Finally, there is the suggestion that planning policies have throttled growth in the cities, an idea which underlies the creation of 'enterprise zones' in inner city areas, where controls are particularly lenient. A number of public policies may have had an impact on urban-rural shifts. Government regional policies are worth consider-

ing in this connection because the urban-rural shift accelerated at the end of the 1950s, at much the same time as regional policy intensified. Two other policies have dealt more explicitly with the distribution of industry within regions. One is the planned decentralisation of people and jobs through overspill schemes and the New Towns programme. The other is the control over industrial development exercised by local authorities through the refusal of planning permission, land-use zoning, and the creation of green belts around larger cities.

Our view is that planning policies have played a minor role in causing the urban-rural shift but are by no means the main motor. Chapter 7, which deals with regional policy, looks in detail at the interrelationship between regional policy and the urban-rural shift and concludes that the acceleration in the shift after 1960 occurred independently of regional policy. The main difficulty with an explanation of urban decline centring on regional policy is that policy has largely distinguished between whole regions, rather than between cities and small towns, whereas the urban-rural shift can be observed in both assisted and non-assisted regions. Other planning policies also fail to account for several characteristics of the urban-rural shift. Firstly, the decline of manufacturing employment in cities is occurring in other Western industrial economies where planning controls are nothing like as highly developed as in Britain. Secondly, despite the great concern to promote economic development shown by many urban authorities in the 1970, employment decline in the cities continued during these years. Thirdly, and most importantly, the remarkably strong association between growth and settlement size does not fit easily with planning controls as they have been operated in this country. For example, though public policies have sought to decentralise people and jobs from London and Birmingham, this has never been an important policy in Clydeside, Tyneside and Merseyside, where high unemployment has meant that the emphasis has been on attracting and retaining industry. Yet as we have noted so often, employment in all conurbations has declined much faster than elsewhere. At the other end of the spectrum, much industrial development in small towns and rural areas has been unplanned, and often even discouraged for environmental reasons. For instance, between 1966 and 1974 over half the industrial movement out of London into the rest of the South East and East Anglia was to locations other than new and overspill towns (Dennis 1978).

Greenbelt policies may, however, have had rather more impact on the urban-rural shift than other planning policies. The creation of areas around major cities where development is largely prohibited has been successful in preventing further urban sprawl, but has also prevented much new industry from locating on the edge of cities, as it did in earlier years. Nowhere has this been more important than in London, where new factories have been diverted beyond the green belt. To this extent physical planning has played a role in encouraging the urban-rural shift, but since greenbelt policies affect only the location of new factories, while urban-rural differences arise mostly from the growth of existing factories, they must remain a minor part of the whole process.

The Role of Constrained Locations

In our view, which will be familiar to the reader by now, the shift of manufacturing out of large cities is occurring because firms find great difficulty in undertaking physical expansion within urban areas. Most existing factories in cities are physically constrained, in that they are hemmed in by urban development, often at high densities, and cannot expand either within their existing sites or onto adjacent ones. At the same time urban sites are unavailable or relatively unsuitable for much new factory building. These characteristics of cities have two crucial consequences.

Firstly, they mean that companies which require extra space, but which operate on sites with no room for expansion, must either forgo the possibility of growth or must undertake some or all of their production in alternative locations—by transferring to a more spacious site or by diverting the extra production to another factory. Since small towns and rural areas offer more room for physical expansion, most new factory floorspace, and the jobs that go with it, are located in these places. This is a well-documented process, which has been spreading industry beyond major cities for many years. The result is a slower growth in cities than elsewhere, though the process does not by itself lead to large job *losses* in uban areas since it concerns the location of increases in production and employment.

Secondly, in urban factories with no room for expansion the rising capital intensity of production, and the associated increase in floorspace requirements per worker, ensure that employment falls. Competitive pressures compel most firms to introduce more capital intensive methods, and thus raise labour productivity, regardless of the extent to which their premises and sites are suited to modern production methods. In a factory where physical expansion is impossible, new machinery displaces labour on the shop floor and leads to a fall in employment. It is this major and rapid displacement of labour by capital which is the driving force behind the *loss* of manufacturing jobs in cities. The same displacement of labour by capital occurs on existing floorspace in small towns, of course, but their losses are offset by jobs created in new factories and factory extensions.

The reasons why new industrial building occurs mostly outside densely built-up areas are not hard to find. Urban land is relatively expensive and sufficiently large sites are difficult to assemble, especially if additional space immediately adjacent to existing premises is required. Even the derelict land found in many cities gives a misleading impression of the room for industrial development, because all too often it is designated for other uses, or blighted by the indecision of planning authorities as in London's docklands. Poor access for heavy lorries, and the official discouragement of urban sprawl, particularly be greenbelt policies, exacerbate the lack of factory building in cities, so that firms now tend to locate new factories in cities only in the few cases where there are compelling advantages to be gained from operating in these locations. In contrast to the formidable barriers to development in urban areas, post-war improvements in transport and accessibility have been important in allowing so much factory building to occur away from cities. Rural locations now suffer little or no disadvantage in transport costs, while telecommunications and the motor car have made rural areas residentially attractive to many people who have been content to follow jobs out of the cities.

The rising capital intensity of manufacturing industry, which is responsible for the large job losses in constrained urban factories, is illustrated by Table 5.20. In the 1950s the growth in capital stock per employee was modest by later standards. Coupled with the greater leniency towards factory building on the edge of cities during these years, this meant that urban manufacturing employment declined only slowly. In the 1960s and 1970s, perhaps under the stimulus of increased foreign competition induced by trade liberalisation, capital intensity accelerated, and since the mid-1960s, when figures have been available, floorspace requirements per worker can also be seen to have risen considerably. The effect has been to accelerate job losses in factories with no room for expansion, which form a high proportion of the total factory stock in major cities. Indeed, in a factory with no possibility of extending its production area, the average rise in floorspace per worker could by itself be expected to reduce employment by one-quarter between 1966 and 1975.

The decline of employment in physically constrained factories and its growth elsewhere are crucial to the urban-rural shift because the

Table 5.20   Changes in capital intensity and floorspace per worker in manufacturing industry 1952–75

	Growth per year in capital stock per employee[1] %	Growth per year in floorspace per employee[2] %
1952–60	3.5	n.a.
1960–66	4.1	n.a.
1966–71	5.5	2.5
1971–75	5.5	4.0

[1] U.K. at constant prices.
Source of capital stock data: National Income and Expenditure blue books.
[2] England and Wales only. Certain establishments such as shipyards and oil refineries are excluded since floorspace is difficult to define.
Source of floorspace data: Abstract of Regional Statistics.

proportion of factories with no room for expansion is likely to increase with the size of a settlement. This is due only in part to the lower density of development in small towns. A more important factor is that in any urban area the factories with room for expansion are most likely to be located at or near the periphery, where existing urban development is not an important constraint, and the proportion of factories in these more peripheral locations is much higher in small towns than in cities. An example makes this clearer. Simple geometry tells us that a circular small town two miles across will have an area of just over three square miles and a circumference (or periphery) of about six and a quarter miles. A city 10 miles across, however, will have an area of nearly 80 square miles—more than twenty-five times larger—but its circumference will be only a little over 30 miles—only five times greater than the small town. In other words, the likelihood of a given factory being in a peripheral location, where there is room for expansion, will be much lower in the city than in the small town.

The same relationship between the area of a settlement and the length of its periphery also means that the proportion of factories in constrained locations will be only marginally lower in a medium-sized city than in a conurbation, but will fall dramatically nearer the small town and rural end of the urban hierarchy. Again, a simple example illustrates this point. If we assume firstly that the number of factories in an urban area is directly proportional to its area, secondly that the number in unconstrained locations is directly proportional to the length of its periphery, and thirdly that in a very large city such as London, 40 miles across, 95 per cent of factories are constrained, we can calculate the proportion of factories in constrained locations in a range of settlement sizes.

Table 5.21 Hypothetical estimates of the proportion of factories in constrained locations

Size of settlement		% of factories in constrained locations
Diameter (miles)	Population[1]	
2	15,000	4
3	35,000	36
4	65,000	50
7	190,000	71
10	400,000	80
20	1,600,000	90
40	6,300,000	95

[1] assumes 5,000 per square mile.

Using these assumptions, Table 5.21 shows that the proportion of factories in constrained locations increases rapidly with population size up to a city of around 400,000, but much more slowly thereafter. This is important because the same non-linear relationship exists between settlement size and employment change. For example, our figures for 1959–75 showed that while the average growth of manufacturing employment in free standing cities was roughly 20 per cent better than in the conurbations, it lagged no less than 70 per cent behind the growth of the most rural areas. In other words, the distribution of constrained locations is capable of explaining not only why employment growth improves as settlement size diminishes, but also why employment growth rises so sharply in the smallest settlements.

In reality not all locations within a built-up area are constrained, although the great majority are likely to be. Similarly, not all peripheral or rural locations will have space for expansion, although the chances are obviously much greater than for urban locations. A unique and detailed study of Birmingham (JURUE 1979) shows the extent of the problem in a major urban area. This study, covering 80 per cent of factories in the city (but excluding the periphery) revealed that 70 per cent of those examined are on sites with no room for expansion, and only 17 per cent have the possibility of expansion within their existing sites. Half of the industrial buildings in this 'core area' of Birmingham completely cover the site they occupy. The building stock exhibits other characteristics which are unsuited to modern industrial production: almost half of the buildings in this area are pre-1914, and two-thirds have their production space spread over two or more floors. Birmingham, which incidentally lost nearly a quarter of its manufacturing jobs between 1971 and 1976, also dispels the myth that vast quantities of factory floorspace are empty or derelict in major cities. Only 8 per cent of the industrial building stock is vacant at any one time—5 per cent on the market, and 3 per cent unoccupied and held off the market. Additions of new floorspace, through development, redevelopments and extensions, have historically been at a rate of approximately one per cent of the existing stock per year—much too low to make any impression on the inadequacy of existing supply—and because so little is built by developers, industrial firms have to rely overwhelmingly on their own efforts to provide this new floorspace.

As JURUE point out, the difficulties in assembling worthwhile industrial sites in conurbations, and their inner areas in particular, mean that additions to the building stock are largely directed away from the areas which exhibit the worst problems of congestion and density, and the investment which does take place in inner areas serves only to perpetuate the existing stock and its poor layout. All in all, the Birmingham study provides a vivid illustration of the physical obstacles to industrial expansion in one conurbation, and there is little reason to suppose the situation is any different in Britain's other large cities.

Testing the Theory
Of course physical constraints are not the sole cause of employment decline. Some factories in unconstrained locations experience declining employment for other reasons, although those in constrained location will usually be unable to expand. However, the balance between constrained and unconstrained locations provides an explanation which can differentiate cities from small towns and rural areas. Moreover, its great strength as an explanation for the urban-rural shift is that it can account for *all* the eight characteristics of the shift which we listed on page 98. Let us consider each in turn.

The strength of the association between manufacturing employment change and settlement size (1) has already been dealt with. As we noted, because cities have a large proportion of their area which is internal and built around, they are likely to have a higher proportion of constrained locations than small towns. The larger the town, the higher the proportion of constrained locations and the worse the employment trends. The international nature of the urban-rural shift (2) reflects the rising capital intensity of production and increase in floorspace requirements per worker which seem likely to characterise all Western economies. As in Britain, in these other countries the proportion of constrained locations is also likely to rise with settlement size.

The acceleration in the urban-rural shift in Britain since the late 1950s (3) probably reflects two factors which intensified the problem caused by the lack of room for expansion in urban factories. The first is the faster rise in capital intensity after 1960, shown in Table 5.20 earlier. The annual rate of increase in capital per worker was 50 per cent higher in the late 1960s and 1970s than in the 1950s, and though we have no information on the increase in floorspace requirements prior to the 1960s, it seems likely that the faster growth in capital intensity also accelerated the increase in floorspace requirements per worker. The second possible factor is the additional restriction on urban industrial expansion posed by planning controls. In particular, the introduction and operation of stringent greenbelt policies around major cities probably speeded the urban-rural shift by further limiting the land available for industrial expansion. Although the legislation underpinning the modern planning system dates from 1947, it seems likely that the implementation of controls took some years to reach its full potential.

The distribution of constrained locations accounts for the mechanisms through which the urban-rural shift is brought about (4). We showed that the location of new jobs—in new and expanded factories—is more important than the location of contractions and closures in differentiating cities from small towns. This happens for a number of related reasons. Firstly, more new branch plants and transferring companies locate outside major cities than within them, for reasons connected with the cost, unavailability and unsuitability of urban land. Secondly, among surviving factories the growing ones contribute more to urban-rural contrasts than the declining ones because the lack of room for expansion ensures that nearly all large additions to employment in existing establishments occur outside built-up areas. The lack of room for expansion in cities does not of course act as an impediment to firms which are declining for reasons unconnected with location, so contractions are more evenly spread. Even so, the loss of jobs through contractions in cities remains a little above average because some firms which might have expanded if room had been available shed jobs as new machinery displaces labour from their constrained factory sites. Thirdly, the urban-rural contrast is relatively small among factories which close, because most closures occur for reasons unconnected with location. Indeed, the relatively modest urban-rural contrast in closure rates suggest that firms experience few, if any, operating cost handicaps in cities, because if costs were markedly higher in cities we would expect to observe much higher closure rates than elsewhere.

As sources of new jobs, the opening of new factories (new firms and new branches) tends to be less important than the expansion of existing establishments, and this is reflected in the relative importance of these two mechanisms in the overall urban-rural shift. Our figures for the East Midlands showed that new branch plants accounted for about one in four of all jobs gains between 1968 and 1975, and over the country as a whole employment in industrial moves (mainly in new branches) accounted for roughly a quarter to a third of the overall urban-rural shift between 1959 and 1975. Little attempt has so far been made to investigate influences on the location of expansion in existing manufacturing plants, but the wealth of research on industrial movement (e.g. Howard 1968; Keeble 1976; Townroe 1979) confirms a close link between movement and expansion. Industries which are experiencing employment growth also experience high levels of industrial movement, and at the level of the firm the need to find room for expansion is generally cited as the main cause of movement.

The poorer growth of firms in cities, irrespective of corporate status (5), reflects the pervasiveness of the constraint posed by the lack of room for expansion in urban factories. Clearly, a factory lacking room for expansion restricts growth on that site, whether the occupant is an independent firm or a branch of a multi-national. The two contrasts which we identified within the population of firms (6 and 7) can nevertheless still be explained. The fact that very small establishments grow as well in cities as in small towns (6) stems from their mobility. Small firms frequently change premises within the same locality as they outgrow their existing factories, but mobility becomes increasingly difficult as size increases, so that firms with over a hundred employees generally opt instead for diverting growth into new branch plants. Thus small establishments are not physically constrained by the urban environment in the same way as the larger establishments, and consequently no urban-rural shift exists among very small firms.

Similarly, the concentration of urban-rural contrasts in industry with high rates of investment (7) reflects the fact that constrained premises pose a problem only to firms which need to invest more than can be accommodated on their existing sites. In industries with low rates of investment, in which floorspace requirements are growing only slowly if at all, the displacement of labour by machinery in constrained locations, and the diversion of output and employment into small towns and rural areas where there is room for expansion, will not occur on anything like the same scale.

The lower profitability of firms in cities (8) may also reflect the problem of constrained premises and sites. There is no compelling reason why the lack of room for expansion in cities should lead to lower profitability, but a plausible explanation would be that cramped urban premises delay or prevent the introduction of new techniques and production processes which existing factory layouts can only accommodate with great difficulty. In the long run the effect would be to undermine productivity and profitability.

One final piece of evidence reinforces the conclusion that physical constraints on the expansion of factory premises in cities are the main cause of the urban-rural shift in industrial location. This concerns London. In most cities and towns the proportion of factories in constrained locations is not known, but we can safely assume that the proportion is close to 100 per cent in London. The density of urban development, the high cost of land and the vigorous restrictions on development on the edge of the green belt ensure that few sizable factories are able physically to expand their premises and sites in the capital. Assuming that all London's factories are constrained in this way, the national rate of increase in floorspace per worker in manufacturing between 1966 and 1975 could have been expected to produce a fall in London's manufacturing employment of 25 per cent, as machinery displaced labour on the shop floor. The actual loss of employment over this period was 34 per cent, but as total manufacturing floorspace actually *fell* in London during those years (as a result of redevelopment and the encroachment of non-industrial uses such as warehousing) this decline in employment is clearly not much greater than that which could have been expected solely on the basis of rising floorspace requirements per worker.

Conclusion

No other trend in industrial location has been as powerful and pervasive as the shift from cities to small towns. It characterises Britain and other Western industrial countries. It is also sufficiently strong to be the main determinant of the regional pattern of growth: rural regions grow while regions dominated by conurbations decline. How this shift is brought about is rather different to what is popularly supposed. Industrial structure has been unimportant; industrial movement, too, can only account for a small part of the shift to small towns. Nor can the blame for the decline of the cities be pinned on any one group of firms, such as the multi-nationals, or externally owned branch plants. In the main, the decline of the cities has occurred because a wide range of existing manufacturing establishments have grown more slowly in cities than in small towns. The available evidence suggests that this slower growth is probably due to a higher proportion of city-based firms finding themselves in locations where they are unable to expand because their factories are hemmed-in by existing urban development. As machinery displaces more and more labour on the shop floor, employment in the city falls, while the lion's share of any growth in employment goes to smaller towns where there is more room for factory extensions and new premises.

These conclusions are important in assessing future trends in the location of employment because they reveal the deep-seated nature of the urban-rural shift. The difficulties posed by the lack of room for expansion facing many urban factories are to a large extent inherent in the nature of the city as a large, complex and densely developed environment, so even vigorous policies to revive its economic base are unlikely to achieve swift success. Equally, the increase in manufacturing floorspace requirements brought about by rising capital intensity—the main motor behind urban decline—is unlikely to disappear in the event of a revival in the fortunes of British industry.

6 The Location of New Firms

So far we have investigated two factors which lead to unequal growth in manufacturing—industrial structure and urban structure. A third structural factor—size structure, or the mix of large and small plants in an area—affects the pattern of employment change because it is the main influence upon the location of new firms. As we will show, towns dominated by large manufacturing plants generate fewer firms, mainly, it seems, because large plants are an inadequate training ground for potential entrepreneurs, and in the long run this undermines their capacity for adaptation and growth.

It is particularly valuable to examine new firms because until recently they were generally ignored. Their contribution to the national economy and their role in generating disparities in growth between different areas were both unknown and neglected. It is probably fair to say that new firms—by which we mean wholly independent new companies—were regarded by most people as things of the past, something which characterised the nineteenth century but not modern-day industry. Suddenly, in the late 1970s the pendulum swung to the other extreme, mainly because of widespread disillusion with the performance of existing larger companies. It has become fashionable, among politicians in particular, to believe that new firms will create the jobs which larger firms have failed to provide, and in doing so will regenerate areas of high unemployment and restructure the economy in the direction of new products and new markets. Yet the sharp change in attitudes and expectations has had nothing to do with a serious evaluation of the role of new firms. This chapter presents some hard evidence.

Job Creation in New Firms
One point which emerged from the last chapter was that in the short run the contribution of new firms to employment growth is modest. In the East Midlands between 1968 and 1975, wholly new manufacturing firms set up during the period provided an increase in manufacturing employment of about 4 per cent—equal to 23,000 jobs or about one in six of all new jobs in manufacturing in the region during those years. This contribution was mainly the result of

Table 6.1   Employment in new firms in Leicestershire 1947−79

	Cumulative employment in post-1947 new firms	as % manufacturing employment
1947	0	0
1956	6,100	3.8
1968	14,800	8.8
1975	27,600	17.0
1979[1]	36,000	23.0

[1] estimate.

the large number of new firms which were set up (1,650 were still operating in 1975) rather than their average employment, which was only 14 people at the end of the period.

For one part of the region, Leicestershire, the data we hold stretch back almost to the last war, so we can also examine the cumulative contribution of new firms over a longer period. As Table 6.1 shows, if a longer view of employment change is taken the role of new firms becomes much more important: firms founded since 1947 probably now account for almost a quarter of all manufacturing jobs in the county. Moreover, the contribution of new firms is actually slightly greater than the Leicestershire figures suggest because they exclude some new firms which started their life as independent companies but were subsequently taken over and now operate as subsidiaries of larger concerns. In Britain as a whole the proportion of employment in post-war new firms is probably not as high. As we will show, there is evidence to suggest that the rate of new-firm formation in Leicestershire may be about 40 per cent above average, so a figure of 15−17 per cent of manufacturing employment in post-war new firms is more likely for the country as a whole. Nevertheless, this remains a substantial share of employment.

There are two reasons why new firms are more important in the long run than over shorter periods. One is that, on average, they experience substantial growth even after their very early years; the other is that a large number of new firms continue to be established. Both these points deserve close examination.

Growth of new firms
A common view of new firms is that they are short-lived, so that their long-term impact on employment is never very great. Table 6.2 looks at the growth between 1968 and 1975 of firms founded during the previous twenty years, and confirms that the loss of jobs through closures is high, particularly among very young firms. We estimate

Table 6.2   The growth of new firms by age: Leicestershire 1968–75

	1968 employment	as % 1968 employment		
		Closures	Net growth in survivors	*Net change*
New 1947–56	5,700	−11.9	+39.5	+27.3
New 1956–68	9,100	−24.5	+50.0	+25.5

that the 1,250 manufacturing firms founded since 1947 which were still operating in Leicestershire in 1975 probably represent no more than a third of all the new manufacturing firms founded in the county between those dates. However, though the loss of jobs in closures is heavy, the growth among surviving new firms is more than sufficient to offset the losses. Table 6.2 demonstrates that as new firms grow older the loss of jobs in closures diminishes and the growth of survivors slackens. But even firms founded in the late 1940s and early 1950s were still on balance adding to their employment in the 1970s.

A proper assessment of the contribution of new firms to employment growth during any period must therefore include not only the jobs in firms set up during that period but also the growth of young firms set up in the immediately preceding years. On this basis, new firms in Leicestershire contributed 13,200 jobs between 1968 and 1975, made up of 9,400 jobs in firms founded during the period and 3,800 jobs from the net growth of firms founded between 1947 and 1968. This was sufficient to add 1.15 per cent a year to the county's manufacturing employment.

The strong growth of young firms is also the cause of the better growth among small firms as a whole, noted in the last chapter, as Table 6.3 demonstrates. Unlike their younger rivals, older small firms actually experience a net decline in employment. This contrast is important from the point of view of policy because it suggests that efforts to assist the small-firm sector are probably better directed at the more dynamic younger element rather than at the sector as a whole. In particular, the poorer performance of old-established small firms indicates that tax concessions to facilitate the continuance of family control are unlikely to aid employment growth.

There is still evidence in Table 6.3 that the rate of growth of firms declines with size, particularly among younger firms. This seems to reflect a 'life-cycle' phenomenon among companies. Firms start small, some grow, but once they have reached a certain size or age

Table 6.3   Employment change in young and old firms by size: Leicestershire 1968–75

Employees in 1968	Net change as a % employment in each group and size band in 1968	
	Firms new 1947–68	Pre-1947 firms[1]
1–25	+40.3	– 1.3
26–100	+22.0	–11.8
101–500	+ 3.8	–19.4
501+	n.a.	–19.0

[1] by size of establishment.

decline sets in. It is hard to say when the watershed comes, but it is worth noting that research has shown that small firms run by first-generation entrepreneurs fare much better than other small firms (Merrett Cyriax Assocs. 1972), so for many firms the period of buoyant growth may be tied to the life of their founder. On the other hand, it must be remembered that not all firms follow this simple life-cycle, and some do continue to grow for many decades.

Despite the healthy growth of many new firms during their first ten or twenty years, it would be wrong to asume that they develop quickly into industrial giants. Fewer than one per cent of all new firms founded in the East Midlands since 1968 employed 100 or more people by the mid-1970s, and only one of these employed more than 250. Moreover, among all the firms founded in Leicestershire since 1947, only the very largest handful employed 400–500 people by 1975. It is perhaps unfortunate that the small firm which grows to be a sizable corporation in a handful of years is the one which usually receives all the publicity, because such firms are extremely unusual. As we have already noted, new firms are an important source of employment because there are a lot of them, not because they are individually very large.

Rate of formation

The second cause of the long-run importance of new firms is the large number which continue to be established. It has sometimes been suggested that higher taxes and increasing paperwork have killed off enterprise and reduced the rate at which new businesses are set up. Again, using our data covering the period since 1947, we can examine the rate at which new firms have been set up during each of three decades. For much of the period our records refer to sur-viviors at certain dates rather than to all new firms, so some firms that survived for only a few years are excluded, but an allowance has been made for these, as described in Appendix A. The results,

Table 6.4   *The formation of new firms by period: Leicestershire 1947–75*

Date of opening	Surviving new firms at end of each period		
	Average emp. at end of each period	No. of firms per year	No. of firms per year on comparable basis[1]
1947–56	12	58	63
1956–68	14	52	63
1968–75	15	91	91

[1] adjusted to allow for different length of each period (see Appendix A).

shown in Table 6.4, are striking. There has been no fall in the rate of new-firm formation. In fact there appears to have been an increase in recent years, and in addition firms founded more recently have grown a little more quickly. This finding casts considerable doubt on the conventional wisdom that rates of personal income tax influence rates of new-firm formation. Despite the steady increase in the burden of income tax since the early 1950s, the rate at which new firms are founded has not fallen, but actually seems to have risen in the 1970s. On the basis of this evidence it seems unlikely that reducing income tax will do much to stimulate the formation of new enterprises.

As a result of surveys undertaken in 1972 and 1979 we also have information (described in Appendix A) on the precise year of foundation for a sample of 210 surviving new firms in the East Midlands. In conjunction with assumptions about rates of survival and closure (also described in Appendix A), the dates of formation of these surviving new firms can be used to produce a unique picture of annual rates of new firm-formation. Figure 6.1, which plots these figures, shows two phenomena. Firstly, there was an immense boom in the formation of new firms in the years immediately following the Second World War. Even the most socialist government Britain has ever had did nothing to dent the vitality of the small business sector of the period. The circumstances during these years—the large number of servicemen being demobilised and the pent-up consumer demand after the war—do, however, make these early post-war years exceptional.

Secondly, there is a marked cycle in new-firm formation. When unemployment is at its worst, new-firm formation seems to be at its highest. The cyclical fluctuations are large: the number of new firms founded in a peak year, such as 1968 or 1972, can be two or three times greater than in a low year, such as 1965 or 1970. The cyclical

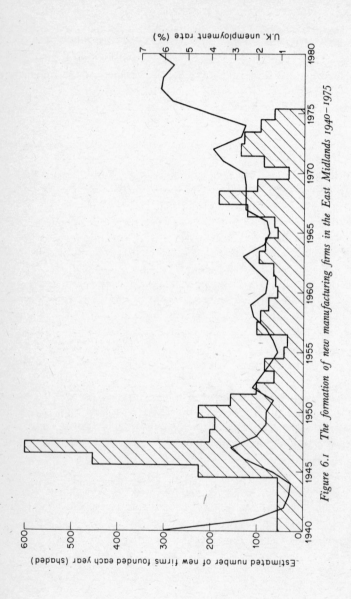

Figure 6.1   The formation of new manufacturing firms in the East Midlands 1940–1975

variation has also been more marked than the long-term increase in rates of new-firm formation which we have already noted. Whatever causes the cyclical fluctuations is clearly a powerful influence, but equally plainly it can have little to do with income tax.

It is not clear why new-firm formation should be so buoyant when unemployment is high and the economy is depressed. One possibility, given that Figure 6.1 is based on information from *surviving* new firms, is that a higher proportion of firms set up during booms are killed off very quickly by the subsequent recession, whereas firms set up during recessions are cosseted by the following upturn and are thus able to get better established. Alternatively, it could be that in the depths of a recession some potential entrepreneurs are able to see the point at which orders will begin to pick up once more, realise that business is about to take a turn for the better, and therefore see it as a good time to start a business. A more plausible explanation for the high rate of new-firm formation during recessions may be that potential entrepreneurs are pushed into starting their own firms either by unemployment or by blocked career prospects with their present employers. Certainly our survey of new firms (described later in this chapter) showed that a small minority of founders had been unemployed immediately prior to starting their own firm, and rather more had found their opportunities for promotion and advancement were blocked so long as they remained with their existing employers, but it is unclear whether this is sufficient to explain the large cyclical upswings in new-firm formation.

The figures for annual rates of the formation of new firms are based on a sample, unlike the figures in Table 6.4, which referred to periods rather than individual years and were based on *all* new firms in one county, so they should be regarded only as rough estimates. The important point, and one not based on samples, is that new-firm formation appears to have risen in the 1970s, not fallen. Furthermore, given that new-firm formation tends to be greater during years of high unemployment, it is quite likely that the current rate of formation is rather higher than it has been for many years. The heavy demand for very small premises reported by many local authorities supports this prediction. What this means for differences in employment change from place to place is that new firms are probably becoming a more important influence on the pattern of unequal growth.

The Location of New Firms

The previous chapter noted that more new firms are set up in rural locations. Within the East Midlands the most rural areas experience

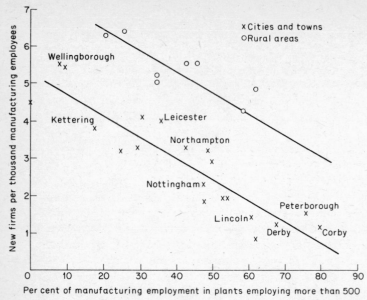

Figure 6.2   New-firm formation by district in the East Midlands 1968–75

a noticeably larger increase in employment from new firms than the cities, and there is additional evidence from Manchester that new firms are even less important in a major conurbation. Figure 6.2, which shows rates of new-firm formation by local authority district in the East Midlands, demonstrates that there are in fact *two* contrasts. Firstly, rates of new-firm formation are higher in rural areas, but secondly this rate declines sharply as the proportion of employees working in large plants increases.

This second contrast between large and small plant towns is very marked, as Table 6.5 shows. The large plant towns in the East Midlands—those with over half of their manufacturing jobs in factories which individually employ 500 or more people—had formation rates little more than a third as high as those in other towns in the region. In the short run this does not matter too much because new firms do not provide many jobs anyway, but in the long run new firms become a substantial source of employment. The low rate of new-firm formation in large plant towns will therefore eventually undermine their capacity for self-sustaining employment growth. At the same time a low rate of new-firm formation removes a vital source of adaptation and diversification in an area's economy and increases dependence on the few major employers who already dominate large plant towns.

Table 6.5   New-firm formation in large and small plant towns in the East Midlands 1968–75

	% of 1968 manufacturing employment in large plants[1]	New firms per thousand employees	% of 1975 manufacturing employment in new firms
Large plant towns[2]	68	1.1	1.7
Other towns	36	3.1	4.4

[1] plants employing over 500.
[2] towns with over 50 per cent of manufacturing employees in plants employing more than 500, i.e. Derby, Peterborough, Lincoln, Mansfield, Loughborough, Corby, Newark.

Later in this chapter we investigate the underlying causes of this contrast, but if for the moment we assume that the relationships shown in Figure 6.2 hold in all areas, it is possible to estimate rates of new-firm formation in other parts of the country. Table 6.6 shows the estimated formation rate for a selection of areas dominated by either large plants or small plants. Leicestershire, as already indicated, has a rate of new-firm formation considerably greater than the estimated national rate, and well above the average for the East Midlands. The estimates in the table are based on the findings for

Table 6.6   Estimated rates of new-firm formation for selected areas

	% of 1972 manufacturing employment in plants employing 500+[1]	Rate of new-firm formation East Midlands = 100
Small plant areas		
Cornwall & N. Devon	16	218
Sussex Coast	22	148
N.E. Lancashire	30	131
Leicestershire	36	130[2]
Hull	44	101
U.K.	48	92
Large plant areas		
South Yorkshire	55	78
West Glamorgan	65	57
Mid Lancashire	67	52
Teesside	68	49
Coventry	72	42

[1] Source: Census of Production 1972.
[2] actual.

the East Midlands, and upon only two contrasts in rates of new-firm formation: between urban and rural areas, and between large and small plant towns. In practice the actual rate of formation will also vary a little from place to place in response to other factors, such as the socio-economic mix, which may affect the supply of potential entrepreneurs. However, confidence in the estimates is increased by the fact that the actual formation rate for Teesside is close to the predicted rate. Robinson and Storey (1981) calculated that between 1965 and 1976 wholly new firms added 1.6 per cent to Teesside's manufacturing employment. On the basis of Figure 6.2, the estimated addition to employment from new firms during this period would be 1.8 per cent.

If the estimates are broadly correct then the contrasts across the country can be large, with some rural areas dominated by small plants, such as Cornwall and North Devon, having a rate of new-firm formation four or five times that of areas such as Teesside and Coventry. The contrasts are not simply between the 'depressed' North and the 'prosperous' South and Midlands. The formation rate in Leicester is over three times as large as the estimated rate for Coventry, little more than twenty miles away. The difference represents a relative loss of about 1,000 jobs a year to the Coventry area. This is unimportant when Coventry's main industries are doing well, as they were in the 1950s and 1960s, but becomes important when the prospects for these industries look bleak, as they do at present.

However, it is in the large plant towns within the development areas that the loss of jobs through low rates of new-firm formation is likely to be most important. Some of the towns with the highest proportion of employment in plants with 500 or more workers are found here—Teesside (68 per cent), Clydeside (56 per cent), Tyneside (59 per cent) and Merseyside (64 per cent). Furthermore, in the last three of these areas the rate of new-firm formation will be depressed not only because they are dominated by large plants, but also because they are conurbations. It is therefore not surprising that Firn and Swales (1978) found that new firms provided only a 1.5 per cent increase in employment in Clydeside between 1963 and 1972.

But if the location of new firms really is important for long-run differences in employment growth it should be possible to identify a disparity in growth between areas dominated by large plants and areas dominated by small plants. To examine this possibility we have divided each type of area in the country as a whole— conurbations, free standing cities, industrial towns and so on—into large and small plant areas. The measure of employment creation

Table 6.7   *Employment generation in large and small plant areas 1959–75*

	Indigenous performance[1] as % of 1959 manufacturing employment	
	Large plant areas[2]	Small plant areas
London	n.a.	−28.7
Conurbations	−11.1	− 2.7
Free standing cities	+ 3.5	+15.5
Industrial towns	+12.9	+20.2
County towns	+ 12.2	+28.9
Rural areas	n.a.	+54.7

[1] manufacturing employment change after allowing for industrial structure and industrial movement.
[2] areas with more than half their manufacturing employment in plants which employ 500 or more (Source: Census of Production 1972).

we have used is 'indigenous performance', a category introduced in the previous chapter. This is the employment change after allowing for industrial structure and industrial movement—in other words the change generated from within each area—which is what we need to look at in order to detect the influence of different rates of new-firm formation. The results, in Table 6.7, are clear enough. Cities grow more slowly than smaller towns and rural areas, but within each type of area employment growth is lower in areas dominated by large plants. This is precisely the pattern we would expect given the association between large plant towns and low rates of new-firm formation.

In areas with a predominance of smaller factories employment grows by between 0.5 per cent and 1.0 per cent a year faster than in areas dominated by large plants. This difference is close to what we would expect on the basis of the contrasts between large and small plant towns in the East Midlands. New-firm formation in Leicester, with only 38 per cent of its manufacturing jobs in plants employing 500 or more, is four times higher than in Derby for example, where the proportion in large plants is 68 per cent. New and young firms added 1.15 per cent a year to Leicester's employment between 1968 and 1975, so we would expect the comparable figure for Derby to be 0.25–0.3 per cent a year—a difference of around 0.9 per cent a year. The contrast between these two towns is a little sharper than most, but it does illustrate the point that the differences between large and small plant areas shown in Table 6.7 can plausibly be explained by disparities in rates of new-firm formation.

Table 6.7 is particularly useful because it separates two influences on unequal growth. Small towns and rural areas grow much faster than large cities, irrespective of whether they are dominated by large or small plants, but at the same time small plant areas grow more quickly in every category. A 40 per cent difference in indigenous growth between a large plant conurbation and a small plant county town, for example, consists of two elements: a difference of about 30 per cent because of the urban-rural shift, and a difference of about 10 per cent because small plant areas have higher rates of new-firm formation. The rural areas gain on both counts because none of them is dominated by large manufacturing plants.

Causes of the Low Rate of New-Firm Formation in Large Plant Towns

The extent to which a local economy is dominated by large plants is the main influence on the rate at which new manufacturing firms are set up. We examined six possible explanations, as follows.

(a) The origin of the founder

It could be that founders are moving out of large plant towns in order to set up their businesses. Previous research has however established that the vast majority of founders start their firms in the area in which they already live and work. An earlier survey of new firms in the East Midlands found that, out of a sample of over 400 firms, more than 80 per cent were set up in locations with which the founders already had strong local associations, and this proportion varied little from county to county, or between industries (Gudgin 1978). The wider generality of this proportion is indicated by Dahmen (1970), who found that 80 per cent of new firms in Sweden had been located in this way. Furthermore, the East Midlands survey revealed that no less than 94 per cent of all founders did not consider alternative locations.

There are good reasons why founders prefer to start their firms in their home area. In particular, a knowledge of local markets and a measure of goodwill from traders and businessmen appears to be crucial in the decision to begin production, and such market knowledge is usually gained through personal contacts which tend to be local. Many firms are begun on a part-time basis, to decrease the risks, while the founder maintains his existing job, and during this formative period local ties are often forged which make a later move unlikely. The very small initial size of most new firms also makes a location near to home quite feasible because the firm's demands for labour and premises are normally sufficiently limited to be met (often through personal contacts again) even in areas with apparent shortages. The problem in large plant towns is therefore that they generate few new firms, not that founders are moving elsewhere.

(b) Industrial mix

Large plant towns may be dominated by industries whose products cannot be manufactured by small firms. As roughly 85 per cent of founders set up their firms in trades in which they have previous experience (Gudgin 1978), potential entrepreneurs from these industries may find it impossible to set up a new firm. For instance, a large proportion of Derby's workforce is employed by Rolls Royce making aero-engines, and Rolls Royce employees would be unable to start their own firms in this capital intensive industry. If we assume that all founders start new firms only in their own industry, we can calculate an expected formation rate for each town in the East Midlands, using average formation rates in each industry in the region as a whole. For the large plant towns this produces the following figures for 1968–75:

Expected number of new firms per thousand employees = 2.3.
Actual number of new firms per thousand employees = 1.1.

The large plant towns have an expected formation rate below the regional average of 2.9, implying that industrial mix may be part of the cause of their low rate of formation, but the actual rate still remains well below the expected.

Moreover, this way of looking at the influence of industrial structure overstates the case. To continue the example, Rolls Royce employees have a range of engineering and managerial skills which can be applied to starting new firms outside the aircraft industry. Industrial structure may play some role, but it is not the whole answer. Indeed, the low formation rate in some industries may be the result of the dominance of large plants in these industries rather than any barrier to entry posed by the particular product and the technology.

(c) Small firms as training grounds for entrepreneurs

Large plants may not provide their employees with the relevant experience for starting a firm, since nearly all new firms are small. Consequently towns dominated by large plants will generate few new firms. As part of our investigation of new-firm formation we conducted an interview survey of 47 new manufacturing firms founded in the East Midlands since 1967, 30 of which were in large plant towns and 17 in Leicester, to provide a contrast. The results of this survey wholly support the hypothesis that employees of existing

Table 6.8 Background of founders of new manufacturing firms

Size of firm (no. of employees)	% of founders from each size band[1]	% of manufacturing employment in survey towns in 1968.	Formation rate 1968–75 per thousand employees
Manufacturing			
1 – 25	26	5	11.9
26 – 100	17	10	4.0
101 – 250	17	14	2.8
251 +	32	71	1.0
Non-manufacturing	8	n.a.	0.2

[1]Source: New firms survey.

small firms are more likely to start their own firms. Table 6.8 shows that, immediately prior to starting up, no fewer than a quarter of all founders had worked in manufacturing plants employing 25 or fewer people. A further third had previously worked in establishments employing fewer than 250, and all the founders from non-manu-facturing firms had also worked in small businesses. In contrast, only one in twenty of the manufacturing jobs in the survey towns were in factories employing 25 or fewer, and less than one in three in all factories employing fewer than 250. Clearly, very small manufacturing companies are spawning new firms from among their employees at high rate—at a rate over ten times as high as that from large plants in fact. Research by Johnson and Cathcart (1979) confirms this result within the Northern Region.

Something in large plants inhibits people from setting up in business. Our survey suggested that the problem in large companies is the limited range of work experience (particularly the lack of contact with customers), security of employment, and the lack of con-tact with other founders who might provide an example to follow. In summary, entrepreneurs need appropriate training, as do peop-le in most skills. Very small firms probably provide the most effective training since the owner sets a direct example to his employees.

That few new firms are set up by people from large plants, wherever they are located, seems to be the main cause of the low rate of formation found in large plant towns. But this is not the whole story. Even after allowing for the fact that most entrepreneurs come from smaller firms, the large plant towns still have noticeably fewer new firms than expected and the small plant towns rather more.

(d)   Labour availability and cost

Data from the Census of Production shows that, on average, small firms pay lower wages than large firms. This may mean that local wage rates are higher in towns dominated by large plants so that small firms in these towns find it difficult to compete for labour. Our survey, however, revealed that wage levels varied, with some new firms paying more and some less than the local going rate. Most firms stressed that low wages lead to a less reliable workforce with high turnover, rather than an inability to recruit at all, and those who did find local wage rates a problem were fairly evenly spread between the large plant towns and our small plant town, Leicester. Moreover, the evidence suggests that if wage rates do have any effect they are likely to affect growth and survival, rather than formation rates, because in the initial stages founders nearly always recruit family, friends and old workmates.

Aside from the question of wage rates, there is little evidence that labour availability varies between the large plant towns and Leicester. Levels of unemployment in both places have been similar over the last decade, and reserves of female labour, measured by the proportion of women of working age who are not in employment, have not differed greatly. However, it was noticeable that all firms found it difficult to get skilled men.

(e)   Subcontracting

Among the firms we surveyed, about 60 per cent of engineering firms and 35 per cent of the others had begun with subcontract orders. Since subcontract work is often put out to local firms, if large plants do not subcontract much of their work (say because of a greater in-house capability) there will be a shortage of initial work of this type for prospective founders within large plant towns. Several founders, including some who had previously been contracts managers within large firms, stated that large firms prefer to give work to bigger and longer-established firms. New firms are in a weak position because they generally lack sufficient quality control facilities, do not have a proven record of reliability, cannot undertake long runs, and have poor quality premises, though these problems can usually be circumvented if the founder is known and trusted. Unfortunately we have no information on the total volume of subcontract work put out by different sizes of firm, or where it goes, but given the importance of these contracts for some new firms, and the subjective evidence, our feeling is that this is a significant, if minor, factor in depressing formation rates in large plant towns.

(f)   Premises

A report published by the Department of Industry (1980) argues that rates of new-firm formation have been depressed by a shortage of small industrial premises. It is possible that a relatively severe scarcity of premises for small firms could be a problem in large plant towns. In fact, we found that the scarcity of cheap premises of the right size is a problem for new firms in all areas. The lack of suitable premises may hinder new-firm formation, though the most enthusiastic and resourceful founders no doubt always find a suitable building, but our survey produced no evidence that the availability of premises, or lack of them, could explain the *difference* in rates of new-firm formation between large and small plant towns. One general comment we did encounter was that new purpose-built 'nursery' units are invariably far too expensive for firms in their earliest stages of development.

The conclusion which we have drawn is therefore that the main reason for the lower rate of new-firm formation in large plant towns is that large manufacturing plants provide an inadequate training ground for potential entrepreneurs. The mix of industries in large plant towns, and the lack of suitable subcontract work, probably also play some part, but these are more minor factors.

Craftsmen and Opportunists

So far we have concentrated on the rates at which new firms are set up, but it is also necessary to know something about their subsequent growth in order to understand the impact on employment. In fact, there is no evidence from within the East Midlands that the early growth rates of new firms differ between towns with high or low formation rates, or between urban and rural areas. Nevertheless, there were large differences in the size of the firms we surveyed, with their current turnover varying from £50,000 per year to £3 million per year, and little of this difference was due to the age of the firms.

Previous studies suggest that performance in the early years is strongly related to the background and education of the founders. A useful distinction is between two types of entrepreneur, the 'craftsman' and the 'opportunist' (Smith 1967). The craftsman tends to have a skilled working-class background and an education not normally extending beyond school. He often founds his firm at a time when few alternative ways of earning a living or using his talents are available. He avoids bank loans, relies on personal

Table 6.9   The growth of new firms by type of founder

Background of founder	Number	Average initial capital in constant prices (£ 1976)	Average annual turnover in constant prices (£ 1979)	Average employment in 1979
Graduates etc.	13	22,000	591,000	26
Other white collar	18	11,000	219,000	15
Manual	16	4,000	193,000	18

Source: New firms survey.

contacts, and has few aspirations for long-term growth in his business beyond that necessary to achieve a comfortable standard of living. The opportunist provides a contrast in almost every sense. His background is usually middle class, and he is often more highly educated. He generally has a wide range of work experience, usually in management and involving marketing and administration, and the ambition to set up his own business is often long-standing. Capital is raised in any way possible, and the opportunist pursues an active policy to search for new products and markets. Not surprisingly, the firms founded by opportunists generally show distinctly better growth.

To a large extent our survey confirmed this split. As Table 6.9 shows, those firms started by people with degrees or equivalent qualifications were begun with larger amounts of capital and had achieved the largest average size by 1979. The 'other white-collar' category includes people who had previously worked in a commercial, managerial or technical capacity, but without higher qualifications, many of whom had begun life on the shop floor. Despite starting with more capital their firms had not grown any faster than those started by 'manual' founders with only shop floor experience. Indeed, though founders from manual backgrounds started with the least capital their firms nevertheless had a good record of creating new jobs.

The major contrast in growth appears to be between those with either degrees or professional qualifications (who are a minority among founders) and the rest. This contrast may be important for 'picking winners', but will only lead to regional growth differences if the incidence of the various categories of founder varies between regions. In fact there are sharp variations in the regional distribution of workers in managerial, professional and technical occupations within manufacturing. Table 6.10 shows that the main difference is between the South East (which has 40 per cent of all

Table 6.10   *Employment in managerial, professional and technical occupations within manufacturing, 1971*

	as % regional employment in manufacturing
London	15.6
Other South East	15.9
East Anglia and South West	12.1
Midlands	11.0
North West and Yorkshire	10.0
Development area regions	9.1
G.B.	11.7

Source: Census of Production.

employees in these occupations) and the remaining regions. Even within these occupational categories it is the highest-status occupations requiring most qualifications which are concentrated in the South East. This is important because we found that three-quarters of founders from large plant backgrounds were in these white-collar occupations, and most were also graduates. Large firms in the South East are therefore likely to generate more new firms than large firms in other regions because the South East's firms have a greater proportion of managerial, professional and technical employees. Moreover, as the firms set up by founders from these backgrounds tend to grow more quickly, the South East is also likely to have a large share of the fastest-growing new firms.

Some of the differences in growth between firms may be due to contrasting amounts of initial capital, but not all. The larger initial investment by graduate founders may reflect their greater accessibility to sources of finance, including greater persuasiveness with the banks, but it also appears to reflect ambition and a realistic appraisal of the importance of starting with sufficient capital. Most founders from shop floor backgrounds rely mainly on limited personal resources because they prefer to minimise risk in a situation where they have difficulty in assessing the likelihood of success or failure. Graduate founders are also more likely to start firms in newer industries with greater growth potential (including electronics) and to manufacture products to their own design instead of undertaking subcontract work to other people's specifications. It is likely to be they who have the largest impact upon their region's industrial structure. Looking back over the last hundered years, it seems possible that the dominance of the South East in many of the new twentieth-century industries was due to the greater supply of potential entrepreneurs with the appropriate backgrounds to exploit the opportunities then existing in electrical goods, pharmaceuticals, aircraft and similar industries.

The Economic Impact of New Firms

One nagging doubt remains about new firms: are they simply taking business away from other local firms? Does an extra job in a new firm mean a job lost elsewhere? To help answer this question we asked where our survey firms sold their products. Table 6.11 shows that 41 per cent of firms served markets largely within the East Midlands. A proportion of employment in these firms probably displaces jobs in other East Midlands firms which sell locally. On the other hand, some of these new firms may be displacing imports into the region, and hence may generate jobs which would otherwise have gone elsewhere, and insofar as they do subcontract work for large local firms they probably produce at low cost and aid local efficiency. Nevertheless, the new firms which sell outside the East Midlands are more likely to represent a net gain in employment for the region. Many of the jobs which they create in the region will be at the expense of competitors elsewhere in the country.

The gain to the British economy as a whole from these young firms looks more limited. Less than a quarter of the firms we surveyed undertook some exporting, and many of these did so only on a limited scale. Therefore if new firms benefit the national economy it is more likely to be by preventing imports and by supplying existing large firms cheaply and efficiently (thereby strengthening those firms' abilities to compete against their foreign rivals) rather than by their direct contribution to exports. However, all the firms which we interviewed were still very young, and it seems likely that the proportion of those firms that export will rise as they become older, larger, and better established.

Table 6.11   *Markets served by new firms*

	Number of firms	Per cent
Mainly local	7	15
Regional	12	26
U.K.	19	40
U.K. plus export	9	19

Source: New firms survey.

Conclusion

As providers of new jobs, it must be stressed that new firms make only a small impact over short periods of say five or ten years. The hopes currently expressed by some politicians that new firms can revive the British economy, and provide employment on the sort of scale needed, are ill-founded. Even if the rate of new-firm formation could be doubled, and assuming that the additional output did not cause any offsetting loss of jobs elsewhere in the economy—both highly unlikely assumptions—industrial employment would be expanded by only perhaps half a per cent a year.

But we have shown that new firms make a substantial contribution to economic development over longer periods, and they play an important part in determining the urban and regional pattern of employment growth. The rate of new-firm formation varies from place to place, largely according to the extent to which local manufacturing employment is concentrated in large plants. This appears to be mainly because large plants do not act as adequate training grounds for entrepreneurs. Much of our evidence on this point has come from one region, the East Midlands, but the contrast between large and small plant areas up and down the country suggests that the same processes are occurring elsewhere, and there is every reason to suppose that the same link between large plant domination and the rate of new-firm formation will be found in other Western industrial countries too.

Size structure remains a modest influence on the pattern of manufacturing employment change. Urban structure, for example, has been a much more dominant influence on industrial location during the last two decades. However, because variations in rates of formation are likely to persist over long periods, and because some new firms mature into substantial enterprises, size structure cannot be neglected as a cause of unequal growth.

Taking a long view of employment change, low rates of formation in places such as Tyneside and Clydeside probably help explain why, when their traditional industries began to decline, they were unable to regenerate their own industrial base, even with substantial government assistance, whereas some other areas with still worse industrial structures, such as West Yorkshire (wool textiles) and Northamptonshire (footwear), have shown greater resilience. Nevertheless, the problem in Tyneside and Clydeside is not that the people living in these areas are lazy or lacking in entrepreneurial spirit. The problem in these places—or in Derby, Loughborough and Lincoln in the East Midlands for that matter—is that their heritage of large manufacturing plants does not provide a suitable environment for generating entrepreneurs and new firms. Almost as a result of their success in generating large-scale industry in the past, these cities and towns are now locked into a situation of increasing dependency on the fate of their remaining large employers or on injections of new industry from outside.

HAROLD BRIDGES LIBRARY
S. MARTIN'S COLLEGE
LANCASTER

7 Regional Policy and Its Impact

The location of manufacturing employment depends not only on private companies and individuals but also on the government. The influence of the government is at its most direct in nationalised industries, but is also exerted on private industry through regional policies, and nowhere is this influence better developed than in the United Kingdom. In the immediate post-war years, and then again since around 1960, successive governments have tried to divert jobs into areas of high unemployment. In this chapter we briefly describe the regional policies pursued in Britain and then evaluate their impact in terms of the number of jobs diverted between regions. As will become apparent throughout the chapter, this task is made easier because we are able to draw heavily upon the existing methods developed by Barry Moore, John Rhodes and Peter Tyler, who have also provided us with much useful data.

Regional Policy in Britain

Though British regional policy had its beginnings in the 1930s, it was never pursued with any vigour until after the war. In the years which followed, the detailed changes in the definition of the assisted areas and in individual policy measures have been numerous, so we will restrict ourselves to a description of the main aspects. A fuller account can be found in Keeble (1976) and McCallum (1979).

So far as the definition of the assisted areas is concerned, until the late 1970s the picture was one of steady expansion and increasing differentiation between areas. The nucleus of the present assisted areas was established immediately after the Second World War when South Wales, Merseyside, North East England, West Cumberland and Clydeside were designated 'development areas'. Separate legislation also provided Northern Ireland with similar assistance. At the end of the 1950s regional aid was extended to more of Scotland and Wales, and also for the first time to parts of Cornwall and Devon. More dramatic changes followed in 1966 when development area status was given to virtually the whole of Wales, Scotland and the Northern Region. In the following year a new category of 'special development areas' was introduced within the existing development areas to deal with the decline of employment in certain coalfields, such as the Welsh valleys and Durham. These special development areas were later extended to cover the whole of Clydeside, Merseyside and Tyneside. In 1970 a further new category was created, the 'intermediate areas', which were eligible for assistance at a lower rate, and though again only a few areas in Yorkshire and Humberside and the North West were designated initially, by 1971 intermediate area status had been extended to cover the remaining parts of these regions which were not already receiving assistance.

By the early 1970s the areas receiving assistance embraced all but the Midlands and the south of England, and included over 40 per cent of all Britain's employed population. On the one hand successive government found it easy to extend regional aid to new areas to appease their critics, but on the other hand they subsequently discovered that it was politically impossible to withdraw aid from any of these areas when unemployment was rising nearly everywhere. The election in 1979 of a Conservative Government, determined to cut public spending, brought changes. Regional aid to Yorkshire and Humberside and the North West has been almost entirely withdrawn, and the assisted areas within Scotland, Wales and the North are now much smaller, so that in total the areas receiving assistance now include only a quarter of the employed population. Indeed, the map of the assisted areas is now not too dissimilar to the one first established in 1945.

The tools of regional policy fall into three broad categories. Firstly, there is the financial inducement provided to companies to move to or expand in the assisted areas. Figure 7.1 shows expenditure on these items at constant prices since 1960/61. Between 1946 and 1960 expenditure on regional policy was low, averaging only £6.4 million per year, but this rose in the early 1960s, and again quite steeply after 1966. Total expenditure fell a little in the early 1970s under a Conservative Government, only to rise again under Labour, but in the late 1970s expenditure was reduced once more, and by 1982 is planned to fall to little more than half its 1978/79 level.

Most of the expenditure on investment incentives is accounted for by Regional Development Grants, and their predecessors, which cover a certain percentage of the cost of new plant and machinery, but discretionary aid (or Selective Financial Assistance as it is known) and financial support from the Scottish and Welsh Development Agencies are becoming more important. Investment incentives are available both to existing firms in the assisted areas, and to firms moving into them. The Regional Employment

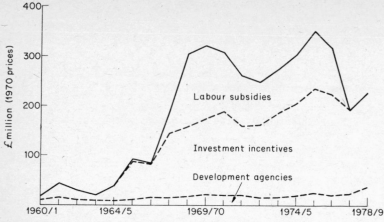

Figure 7.1   Expenditure on regional policy 1960/1 – 1978/9
Source: Moore, Rhodes and Tyler (1980)

Premium (REP) introduced labour subsidies into the regional policy package in the late 1960s. All firms in development areas became entitled to a flat rate subsidy, based on their total number of employees, but the decision in 1976 to abolish REP (except in Northern Ireland) meant that all forms of regional aid to companies once more became geared to encouraging investment rather than employing more labour.

The second tool of regional policy has been the control over factory building, initially by building licences and subsequently through Industrial Development Certificates (IDCs), which firms must obtain in order to build or extend a factory above a certain minimum size. Figure 7.2 shows the strength of IDC policy, measured by the number of jobs associated with IDC refusals in the South East and Midlands expressed as a percentage of the 'expected' employment associated with all applications in these regions. The strength of IDC control fell during the 1950s, but was increased in the early 1960s and for a period was quite stringent. In the 1970s IDC control was eased once more, so that it is currently no stronger than during the 1950s.

IDC control has a lot to recommend it because it is simple to operate and costless to the Exchequer (except for small administration expenses). On the other hand, there is no guarantee that the factories for which permission is refused in the South and Midlands will necessarily find their way to the assisted areas, and IDC control also runs the risk of slowing industrial investment or causing some projects to go abroad or to be shelved altogether. Furthermore, such

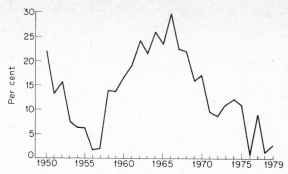

Figure 7.2   The strength of IDC policy as measured by 'expected employment associated with refusals' as a percentage of 'employment associated with approvals plus refusals' in the South East and Midlands regions.
Source: Moore, Rhodes and Tyler (1980)

a direct means of diverting employment inevitably generates opposition in the losing area at times when unemployment is high by post-war standards. It is therefore not surprising that in the more depressed economic conditions which now prevail, when the emphasis is on securing as much industrial investment as possible as soon as possible, IDC control is regarded as a largely inappropriate arm of regional policy.

The third tool of regional policy has been heavy investment in infrastructure in the assisted areas. Some of this has been directly related to the attraction of industry, such as investment in trading estates and factory building, but a great deal has also gone into roads, housing and city-centre redevelopment in the hope that a higher standard of provision in these items will in the long run improve the attractiveness of the assisted areas to new industrial development.

Most of the efforts to raise employment in the assisted areas have been directed towards manufacturing industry. The implicit assumption has been that most service activity depends on the manufacturing base—a conclusion which the analyses in Chapter 3 confirmed—though disillusion with the likely achievements of a policy based on manufacturing alone has shifted the balance a little in recent years. Small grants are now available to some service firms which relocate in assisted areas, and central government has moved some of its offices out of London and the South East, though civil service dispersal has now come to an end. The overwhelming share of expenditure on regional policy, and the political emphasis, nevertheless continue to be on manufacturing.

In addition to explicitly 'regional' policies, a number of national economic policies have also provided assistance to specific regions, often as one of their main objectives. The Temporary Employment Subsidy, for example, introduced in 1975 to prevent redundancies, has in effect served as a subsidy to the North West, Yorkshire and Humberside, and the East Midlands, where the take-up has been high in ailing textile industries. The sustained support which the shipbuilding industry has received over the years, culminating in nationalisation in 1976, must also be interpreted as an effort to preserve jobs in some of the areas experiencing severe unemployment.

Problems in Measuring the Effects

The efforts to shift jobs into areas of high unemployment have therefore been substantial during the last two decades, but because the current problem areas are little different from those of 1945—places such as South Wales, Tyneside and Clydeside—one could be forgiven for assuming that thirty years or more of regional policy has really been thirty years of wasted effort. In fact there is good evidence that regional policy has had considerable success in raising employment in the assisted areas.

Figure 7.3 shows that manufacturing employment in the four 'development area regions' which received the bulk of the assistance—the Northern Region, Scotland, Wales and Northern Ireland—declined relative to the national average up to the early 1960s, but then improved dramatically. All four of these regions show such an improvement, which coincides with the intensification of IDC control and an increase in expenditure on regional aid at about the same time. However, in the mid-1970s their relative growth began to tail off, and there is some evidence that the downward trend of the 1950s may have resumed. Nevertheless, though the superficial picture in Figure 7.3 shows that the

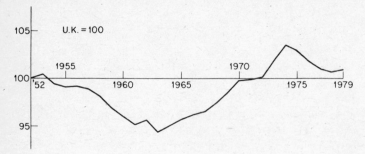

Figure 7.3   Manufacturing employment change in Scotland, Wales, Northern Ireland and the Northern Region relative to the U.K.

development area regions as a whole have not done too badly, it does not prove that regional policy has worked. What needs to be established is what would have happened *in the absence of regional policy.* The correct measure of the impact of regional policy is the difference between what actually happened to manufacturing employment in the assisted areas and what would have happened anyway without regional policy.

Moore and Rhodes (1973), and later with Tyler (1977, 1980), have made considerable progress in disentangling the impact of regional policy. Their starting point is the difference between regional employment trends in the 1950s, when regional policy was virtually inoperative, and in subsequent years when policy was actively pursued. They also argue that the appropriate measure of regional trends is the employment change after allowing for the influence of industrial structure, or the differential shift as we called it in Chapter 4. Moore, Rhodes and Tyler assume that if regional policy had not been intensified in the 1960s and 70s, the rates of differential shift in the assisted areas would have been the same as during the 1950s. This enables them to calculate the employment change in the assisted areas which they believe would have occurred after 1960 in the absence of regional policy, and they attribute the difference between this expected change and the actual change to the impact of those policies. In addition, they make adjustments for three more minor factors:

1. The effort of the trade cycle is excluded. They estimate that for every one per cent rise in unemployment above its 1950s' average there is a differential decline in the four development area regions of 10,000 jobs.
2. Employment change in metal manufacturing and shipbuilding is excluded because these industries have been subject to special schemes of assistance.
3. An estimated 20,000 jobs in Scottish manufacturing attributable to North Sea oil developments are excluded from their estimates for 1976.

Using these methods, Moore, Rhodes and Tyler estimate that between 1960 and 1976 regional policy increased manufacturing employment in the four development area regions by 280,000 jobs. The rate at which jobs were being created by policy rose to a peak in the late 1960s, when the development area regions benefited both from continuing intensive policy measures, and from the build-up of employment in firms which had moved to these regions as a result of policy in the early 1960s. In the 1970s however, the effectiveness of policy has declined. Moore, Rhodes and Tyler estimate that all four development area regions have benefited substantially, though Scotland and Wales have received rather more jobs than the other two. Using broadly similar methods (but excluding any adjustment for the trade cycle) MacKay and Thomson (1979) indentified an improvement in the differential shift up to 1973 of roughly 190,000 jobs, which is roughly in line with the findings of Moore, Rhodes and Tyler. On the basis of these figures, it seems that regional policy has resulted in a considerable increase in employment in the assisted areas.

Moore, Rhodes and Tyler's methods form the basis for our own estimates of the impact of regional policy, but require some important modifications. The major difficulty in measuring the impact of regional policy on employment is that the other influences on employment change must be successfully disentangled. In the previous chapters we outlined three underlying causes of unequal growth in manufacturing—industrial structure, urban structure and size structure. Only the first of these, industrial structure, is fully unravelled in the Moore, Rhodes and Tyler estimates. The other two causes would affect the estimates of the impact of regional policy if their influence upon employment changed in magnitude before and after 1960, and thus altered underlying regional trends. Chapter 6 showed how the size structure of industry in an area—the mix of large and small manufacturing plants—affects employment growth because areas dominated by large plants generate few new firms. As there was some evidence that the rate of new-firm formation rose in the 1970s, the disadvantage of large plant towns has probably worsened, but this is unlikely to influence the estimates of regional policy because new firms account for so few jobs over a short period of time.

The same cannot be said of the influence of urban structure. There is evidence that the relative decline of the large cities, and of London in particular, began in earnest at around the same time as regional policy was intensified at the end of the 1950s. Any comparison of the period of 'active' policy after 1960 with the earlier 'passive' policy years consequently runs the risk that changes brought about by the increased urban-rural shift may be wrongly attributed to regional policy. This point is illustrated by Table 7.1, which compares the two periods in both assisted and non-assisted regions. The improvement in the trend in the three development area regions is clearly visible after 1960 and is usually ascribed to regional policy. However, the same improvement occurred at the same time in the three non-assisted regions shown in Table 7.1. The

Table 7.1   Manufacturing employment change adjusted for industrial structure[1] by period 1952–79

	as % 1960 manufacturing employment			
	'Passive' regional policy 1952–60	'Active' regional policy		
		1960–66	1966–73	1973–79
Development area regions[2]	−1.7	+2.9	+ 7.0	0.0
Less urban southern regions[3]	+4.1	+5.7	+11.1	+7.0

[1] differential shift (1960 base year, 77 industry disaggregation).
[2] North, Scotland, Wales.
[3] East Anglia, East Midlands, South West.
The assisted areas in the South West and East Midlands contained 5 per cent and 3 per cent respectively of total manufacturing employment in each region in 1960.

important point is that these three non-assisted regions all lack a conurbation, and in each case manufacturing is located in smaller cities, towns and rural areas. This meant that they not only had an advantage over more urban regions, but also had an advantage which increased after 1960. What we now need to do is to look at the extent to which the acceleration in the urban-rural shift occurred independently of regional policy, and then at its implications for the estimates of the impact of regional policy itself.

Regional Policy and the Urban-Rural Shift

London and the other conurbations were losing jobs slowly in the 1950s, but Table 7.2 shows that this rate of loss—measured by the

Table 7.2   Manufacturing employment change adjusted for industrial structure[1] by type of area

	as % per year of 1961 manufacturing employment	
	1951–61	1961–76
London	−0.6	−2.4
Conurbations[2]	−0.6	−1.0
Free standing cities[2]	−0.4	−0.1
Hinterlands	+0.7	+1.5

[1] differential shift, calculated at SIC order level of disaggregation.
[2] definitions are not comparable with our own classification of areas. See Appendix B.
Source: Moore, Rhodes and Tyler (1980).

Table 7.3   Urban-rural contrasts in assisted and non-assisted regions 1959–75

		as % 1959 manufacturing employment		
		Industrial[1] movement	Indigenous performance	*Differential[2] shift*
London		−12.1	−28.7	−40.8
Conurbations and free standing cities	Development area[3]	+ 9.9	− 6.6	+ 3.3
	Non–D.A.	− 1.9	− 0.1	− 2.0
Other areas	Development area[3]	+15.3	+20.6	+35.9
	Non–D.A.	+ 4.0	+21.6	+25.6

[1] estimates based on Department of Industry figures
[2] 1959 base year, 99 industry disaggregation.
[3] defined as the North, Scotland, Wales (less South Coast, North Coast and North East), Merseyside, South West (Western), Furness.

differential shift—increased dramatically during the next fifteen years, particularly in London. The increase in the rate of loss amounted to 26,000 jobs a year from London and 9,000 jobs a year from the other conurbations. The free standing cities showed a slight improvement after 1960, but the main improvement occurred in small towns and rural areas outside the main cities. Was this acceleration in the urban-rural shift simply the result of regional policy, which was intensified at about the same time?

The first point to note is that urban-rural contrasts in differential growth characterise both assisted and non-assisted areas. Indeed, Table 7.3 shows that the contrast between urban and rural areas is much larger than the contrast between assisted and non-assisted regions. However, the table does show that industrial movement—one of the factors contributing to the differential shift—has favoured both urban and rural parts of the development areas, mainly at the expense of London, and to a lesser extent at the expense of other cities in the non-assisted regions. Certainly, a major change in the pattern of movement did occur at around the time regional policy was intensified. Prior to 1960 the dominant flow of jobs in moves was out of London and into the rest of southern England, and into the Outer Metropolitan Area in particular. After 1960 many of these moves were diverted to the development areas.

Nevertheless, there is no evidence that the movement of firms to the development areas led to an acceleration in the urban-rural shift. This is demonstrated by Table 7.4, which compares net industrial

Table 7.4   Employment in industrial moves by type of area 1952–9 and 1960–75

| | as % per year of 1959 manufacturing employment | |
	1952–9[1]	1960–75[2]
London	−0.91	−0.76
Conurbations and free standing cities	+0.13	+0.09
Other areas	+0.50	+0.38

[1] employment in 1966.
[2] employment in 1975.
Movement figures are estimates based on Department of Industry data.

movement in the passive policy years in the 1950s with the active policy period since 1960. It is difficult to make a precise comparison because the employment figures for the firms which moved in the 1950s relate to 1966, and thus include some build-up to 'mature' employment levels which is excluded from the figures for 1960–75 moves (for which the employment figures relate to 1975). Moreover the sub-regional boundaries which were used to compile the statistics differ, and prevent anything but a comparison of fairly broad urban and rural categories. But the picture is clear enough: the *movement* of industry to small towns and rural areas did not become any faster after 1960.

If the acceleration in the urban-rural shift was not due to factory movement, by implication it must have been due to the emergence of greater disparities in the growth of indigenous industry. More specifically, the acceleration in the shift must have been due to a dramatic worsening of employment trends in London's firms, because it was the increase in job losses in London, rather than the other conurbations, which accentuated the relative growth of small towns and rural areas after 1960. Table 7.3 showed that after 1960 good indigenous growth characterised small towns and rural areas in both assisted and non-assisted regions, but by itself this evidence does not rule out the possibility that regional policy was the cause. What may have happened is that the stringent application of IDC control in London led to a sharp fall in its manufacturing employment and a corresponding boost to indigenous industry in small towns and rural areas, both inside and outside the development areas. There are two channels through which this diversion of jobs could have occurred. Firstly, some firms may have switched the growth bottled-up by IDC control in London into their existing plants in small towns and rural areas. Secondly, if some of the planned expansion prevented by IDC control in London was abandoned by the firms concerned, the main beneficiaries may have been their competitors in small towns and rural areas.

However, the downturn in manufacturing in London seems to have little to do with IDC control. Figures collated by the Department of Industry show that between 1960 and 1976 the employment associated with IDC refusals in London averaged only 1,150 jobs a year, and the figure never rose above 2,500 in any one year even when strong IDC control was applied in the mid-1960s. During the same period the differential decline of London averaged no less than 40,000 jobs a year. It could still be argued that the very existence of IDC control in London deterred industrial expansion, so that refusals alone are a poor guide to the impact of IDC policy. There can be no doubt, for instance, that the tentative enquiries made by some firms indicated that their schemes for expansion in London were unlikely to obtain approval, and that this caused them to divert growth elsewhere. But this too is unlikely to account for much more of London's decline unless we can assume that the jobs lost in this way exceeded those lost through IDC refusals by a factor of 10 or 20. Furthermore, it is worth remembering that IDC applications have always been more likely to succeed than fail. Even during the years when IDC control was pursued energetically, the jobs associated with approvals in the South East and Midlands outnumbered the jobs associated with refusals by more than two to one.

The acceleration in the urban-rural shift after 1960 therefore seems to have little to do with regional policy. Over the country as a whole, industrial movement into small towns and rural areas did not increase after 1960 even though regional policy had a discernible impact on the pattern of movement. Nor can the decline in the performance of London's firms—the key factor in accentuating the relative growth of small towns and rural areas—be blamed on IDC control. Indeed, Chapter 5 argued that the acceleration was probably caused by a sharp increase in the floorspace requirements of manufacturing industry, higher investment in the 1960s, and to a lesser extent the impact of local planning controls.

The effect of the acceleration in the urban-rural shift on employment trends in the four development area regions can be calculated fairly easily, given the proportion of each region's manufacturing employment in conurbations, free standing cities and hinterlands, and the change in the trend in each type of area in the country as a whole after 1960. The estimated decline in these four regions resulting from the small deterioration in the conurbations is more than offset by the estimated boost to their employment caused by the sharp improvement in the growth of small towns and rural areas. We calculate that by 1979, manufacturing employment in the development area regions was 90,000 higher as a result of the increase in the urban-rural shift. Roughly 40,000 of these jobs were in Wales, 20,000 each in Scotland and the North, and 10,000 in Northern Ireland. These jobs must be deducted from the improvement in the employment trends in the development area regions in order to make an accurate assessment of the impact of regional policy.

On a cautionary note however, two assumptions in these estimates must be emphasised. Firstly, we have assumed that after 1976 the urban-rural shift continued at the same rate as between 1971 and 1976, though there is no direct evidence as yet for the second half of the 1970s. Nevertheless, even if the urban-rural shift stopped altogether after 1976—which is most unlikely—this would only be sufficient to reduce the estimated boost to the development area regions from 90,000 to 80,000 jobs. Secondly, we have assumed that the acceleration in the urban-rural shift affected each individual city, town and rural area to the same extent as the average for its 'type', irrespective of where in the country it is located. Since the development area regions are in peripheral locations this assumption must be considered further. Much of the acceleration resulted from the decline of London. The important question is therefore where these jobs went. Our assumption implies that the increased relative decline of London was offset by relative growth in small towns and rural areas up and down the country rather than just in the counties surrounding the capital. There is some justification for this view, because the acceleration in London's decline was not due to an increase in out-movement, but to greater job losses in the firms which remained. Some of these losses may have involved intra-company transfers of production to existing plants in the counties surrounding London, but much of the increased loss must reflect the poor growth of London's companies compared to their competitors elsewhere in the country, and there is little reason to suppose that these competitors are overwhelmingly concentrated in the rest of southern England. Therefore our assumption may not be too inaccurate.

The Impact of Regional Policy

The most important modification which must be made to Moore, Rhodes and Tyler's estimates of the impact of regional policy is the inclusion of an allowance for the effect of the acceleration in the urban-rural shift. There are three other minor modifications that

Table 7.5   Estimated impact of regional policy on manufacturing employment 1960–79

	Thousands				
	1960–6	1966–73	1973–9	Total	(as % 1960)
North	14	50	−12	52	(11.1)
Scotland	30	25	2	57	(7.4)
Wales	13	35	5	53	(17.8)
Northern Ireland	10	11[1]	1[2]	22	(11.8)
Total	67	121	− 4	184	(10.8)

[1] to 1971 only.
[2] employment in 1976 in moves in 1972–6.

have been incorporated in our estimates:

1.   The adjustment for industrial structure is conducted at a finer level (77 groups of industries) using 1960 as the base year.
2.   No adjustment for the trade cycle is included because we find no evidence of cyclical fluctuations in employment in the development area regions during the 1950s when regional policy was inactive.
3.   An allowance for the build-up of employment in firms which moved to the Development Areas in the 1940s is included.

The last of these deserves a word of explanation. The trends between 1952 and 1960 are a misleading guide to underlying trends in the absence of policy—quite apart from any consideration of the changing urban-rural shift—because they include the once-and-for-all build-up to 'mature' levels of employment in firms which moved to the development area regions during the years of exceptionally active regional policy between 1945 and 1951. We estimate (see Appendix A) that the continuing build-up of these policy-induced moves after 1952 added 25–30,000 jobs to the development area regions. These jobs ought properly to be attributed to regional policy, and must be excluded when making an assessment of trends in the 1950s in the absence of any policy effect. Their exclusion lowers the average annual differential shift in the development areas in the 1950s. As the trend in the 1950s is used to calculate what would have happened in the absence of regional policy, the effect of the allowance for build-up is to increase the size of the improvement which can be attributed to regional policy after 1960.

Estimates of the impact of regional policy, based on our modifications of the Moore, Rhodes and Tyler approach, are shown in Table 7.5. Taking the period as a whole, regional policy has raised manufacturing employment in the four development area regions by around 185,000 jobs. The impact of policy has therefore been substantial. The North, Scotland and Wales have gained roughly the same number of jobs, and Northern Ireland considerably fewer. In relation to the existing employment in each region the impact has been uneven: the gain in Wales has been over twice as large as in Scotland. We have not investigated why regional policy has benefited some regions more than others, but there are at least two possible explanations. One is that, because so many of the new branch plants set up in assisted areas originated in the South East and Midlands, firms have preferred to locate close-by in Wales rather than in Scotland, which is considerably more remote from southern England. The other possibility is that many mobile firms prefer to locate in small towns, so that Scotland and the North, which contain conurbations, have not received as many moves as Wales in relation to their size.

Regional policy has also raised employment in the assisted areas outside the four development area regions. Recent estimates suggest that by 1976 policy-induced moves provided 25–35,000 jobs in Merseyside, 18–20,000 jobs in the South West development area (Cornwall and parts of Devon) and 15–16,000 jobs in the Yorkshire and Humberside and North West intermediate areas (Moore, Rhodes and Tyler 1980). Thus regional policy has probably raised manufacturing employment in all assisted areas in total by between 200,000 and 300,000 jobs. Taking all areas together, around 250,000 manufacturing jobs would be a plausible mid-range estimate.

Is Regional Policy Still Working?

From the point of view of policy makers, what is important is not whether regional policy has worked in the past but whether it is still effective today. In answer to this last question Table 7.5 presents some apparently alarming information: after 1973 no regional policy effect can be detected. We are not alone in reaching this conclusion. Keeble (1980, p. 957) also concluded, from a regression analysis of differential shifts by county between 1971 and 1976, that regional policy 'had ceased by 1976 to exert a measurable impact on the geography of manufacturing employment change in Britain'. Despite the millions which continue to be poured into regional aid, is regional policy really now having no effect?

It is not difficult to explain why regional policy should now be less effective. IDC control has been relaxed and the Regional Employment Premium (REP), which accounted for about half of all regional policy expenditure, has been abolished. The depressed economic conditions prevailing since the early 1970s have substantially reduced the level of potentially mobile investment, so that few new branch plants are available to move to the assisted areas, and even those which do find their way to assisted regions are tending to employ fewer people as manufacturing industry becomes increasingly capital intensive.

Alternatively, it could be that the method of estimating the policy effect has simply become inaccurate or inappropriate. The severe depression since the early 1970s may have caused an exceptional loss of jobs in the assisted regions, over and above any decline caused by structural problems. Certainly, some of the jobs which were created in the assisted areas by regional policy will now be beginning to disappear—through the closure of branch plants which moved to these regions in the 1960s, for example. There might also have been a down-turn in the underlying employment trends in these regions in the late 1970s, perhaps caused by the rise in earnings relative to the U.K., which has occurred in Scotland and the North in particular. Changes such as these could hide any continuing regional policy effect. Nevertheless, unless job losses from these sources have been unexpectedly large, the conclusion must be that regional policy has not been very successful in recent years. This does not necessarily mean that it should be abandoned. What the evidence does suggest is that traditional policy tools, which rely heavily on attracting the in-migrant branch plant and favour capital intensive investment, are probably inappropriate in the present depressed conditions.

Regional Policy and Industrial Movement

A further issue of some relevance is the extent to which regional policy has worked by raising the level of industrial movement into the assisted areas or by improving the performance of indigenous industry. Figure 7.4 shows that industrial movement (transfers and new branches) into the development area regions was at a high level during the years of active regional policy in the late 1940s, but fell to low levels in the 1950s. As policy intensified again the number of moves began to rise, reaching a peak in the late 1960s, but in the 1970s movement has fallen once more. Table 7.6 shows that there is also a close correspondence between the level of movement into the four development area regions and our estimates of the total regional policy effect.

Of course, some of these moves would have occurred anyway. Moore and Rhodes (1976) estimate that at least 80 per cent of the

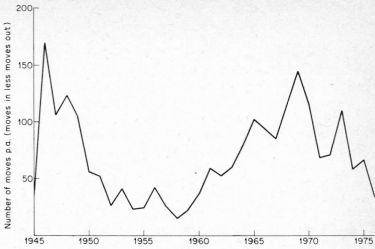

Figure 7.4 Net industrial movement into Scotland, Wales, Northern Ireland and the North 1945-76

moves to development areas, including Merseyside and the South West development area, between 1960 and 1971 can be attributed to regional policy, and that these policy-induced moves accounted for 161–180,000 jobs in 1971. Using the same data, Ashcroft and Taylor (1979) put the figures rather lower, at not much more than 50 per cent of moves, and around 100,000 jobs. Both competing estimates use regression analysis and allow for changes in the national economy as well as changes in the strength of regional policy tools. The disparity occurs mainly because of the ways in which the two sets of estimates allow for changes in the level of economic activity and investment in the economy as a whole.

Moore and Rhodes attribute roughly 60 per cent of the

Table 7.6 Regional policy effect and industrial movement by region 1960-75

	Estimated regional policy effect 1960–75	Net industrial movement[1] 1960–75
North	64	49
Scotland	50	59
Wales	45	47
Northern Ireland	22	32
	181	182[2]

[1] estimates based on Department of Industry figures.
[2] excludes 5,000 jobs which moved between D.A. regions.

employment in policy-induced moves to IDC control alone, and a further 30 per cent to investment incentives. Their findings suggest that REP played a relatively minor role in attracting moves to the development areas, which is perhaps not surprising given that the bulk of REP payments went to existing manufacturing firms in the development areas rather than to in-migrant plants. Ashcroft and Taylor also conclude that both IDC control and capital subsidies have had a substantial effect on the movement of industry, but they find that the main effect of IDC control has been to increase the total volume of movement, while capital subsidies have induced a greater proportion of movers to locate in development areas.

Neither Moore and Rhodes nor Ashcroft and Taylor include an allowance for the effect of motorway building on levels of movement into the assisted areas. At first sight this is surprising because the construction of new roads has always been regarded as one of the main tools of regional policy and has absorbed large amounts of money since the early 1960s. However, the evidence supports the view that whatever its effect on traffic flows, road building does not have much impact on regional development. This is mainly because transport costs are such a small proportion of firms' total costs: almost three-quarters of British industry incurs total transport costs which amount to less than three per cent of the value of gross output (Gudgin 1978). Consequently, even though many road schemes in the assisted areas came to fruition in the mid-1970s, this provided an insufficient attraction to maintain industrial movement into those regions at the same high levels as in previous years. Taking a wider view of growth and decline, it is also noticeable that in the two regions where manufacturing has grown most rapidly, East Anglia and the South West, the road network remained largely unimproved until the end of the 1970s, which suggests that easy access to motorways is certainly not an essential pre-condition for economic development. -

Nevertheless, the fact remains that over half of the overall regional policy effect has occurred through industrial movement, even if road building has had little to do with this movement. The *origins* of the moves to the development area regions can therefore provide some indication of the regions which have lost jobs as a result of regional policy. Table 7.7 shows that the South East has been the most important source of employment in moves, both in absolute terms and in relation to its size. The West Midlands has also provided quite a few jobs, but movement has not been substantial from any of the remaining regions.

The jobs which are diverted to the development areas are not

Table 7.7 Origin of employment in moves to the North, Scotland, Wales and Northern Ireland 1960–75

Origin	Employment in 1975 thousands[1]	as % 1975 manufacturing employment
South East	84	4.0
Abroad	36	n.a.
West Midlands	25	2.3
North West	12	1.1
East Midlands	11	1.9
Yorkshire & Humberside	10	1.3
South West	3	0.7
East Anglia	2	0.9
	182[2]	2.9

[1] estimates based on Department of Industry figures.
[2] excludes 5,000 jobs which moved between D.A. regions.

necessarily 'lost' in the region of origin. In some cases labour shortages might prevent this expansion occurring in the region of origin. In other cases out-movement may release labour, permitting the expansion of other firms held back by labour shortages. It is also possible that in periods of full employment in prosperous regions, the out-movement of jobs may ease the shortage of labour in these areas enough to enable the government to reflate the national economy and thus create more jobs throughout the country. All this is of little relevance after 1966 of course, when unemployment began to rise everywhere and when the national economy became increasingly constrained by the balance of trade rather than labour shortages in certain regions. Nevertheless, even if there were no offsetting job gains in the prosperous regions, Table 7.7 shows that the loss of jobs in moves to the development areas has not hit any region too hard. Even in the South East, which provided so many of the moves, the loss was small relative to its total manufacturing employment.

Conclusion

Regional policy has had a substantial impact on industrial location in Britain. The estimates presented in this chapter suggest that since 1960 it has probably diverted some 250,000 jobs to the assisted areas of which roughly 185,000 jobs in total went to the four development area regions—Scotland, Wales, the North and Northern Ireland. These figures are somewhat lower than other, earlier estimates because part of the improvement in the assisted regions after 1960 must be attributed to the quickening shift of industry towards smaller cities and towns, which occurred at much the same time as regional policy was intensified and which benefited these regions. There is also evidence that regional policy is now having a much smaller impact, as national economic conditions become less favourable and as regional policy itself is pursued less vigorously.

8 Unequal Growth in Manufacturing

The principal finding of this study is that the pattern of unequal growth in manufacturing employment is largely determined by the combined influence of four factors—industrial structure, urban structure, size structure and regional policy. The nature and strength of these factors have been described in the previous four chapters. This chapter examines their relative importance and shows how together they generate the overall pattern of change. The first part of the chapter demonstrates how different levels of employment change in each U.K. region result from the combined action of the four factors, and how the importance of each factor in any region depends on that region's particular characteristics. The second part of the chapter looks more closely at two counties, Cleveland and Leicestershire, to illustrate how sharply-contrasting structural characteristics affect employment change in different ways. These counties grew at similar rates during the period which we examine, but for completely different reasons. The detailed analysis of these two areas suggests that their growth rates are likely to diverge sharply in the future, and provides a good example of how an understanding of the influences upon employment change provides a much greater insight into future changes than a simple extrapolation of past trends.

Regional Employment Accounts

For each region we have assembled 'employment accounts', in Table 8.1, which show how the four factors we have examined contributed to net changes in manufacturing employment between 1960 and 1975. The employment change associated with each factor has been calculated on the basis of the evidence presented in earlier chapters and the detailed estimation procedures are described in Appendix C. The accounts measure the importance of each factor in causing divergences from the national rate of employment change. A negative contribution attributable to size structure, for example, indicates a high proportion of employment in large plants, resulting in a rate of new-firm formation below the national average. While there is inevitably a degree of error in all the estimates, given the information available and the assumptions it has been necessary to

Table 8.1 Employment accounts for manufacturing by region 1960–75

| | | | | | | | | | | as % 1960 manufacturing employment | |
	East Anglia	Wales	South West	North	East Midlands	West Midlands	Scotland	Yorks and Humberside	Northern Ireland	South East	North West
National change	−12.0	−12.0	−12.0	−12.0	−12.0	−12.0	−12.0	−12.0	−12.0	−12.0	−12.0
Difference due to:											
Industrial structure	+ 3.8	+ 0.5	− 3.4	− 3.1	− 1.8	+ 4.7	− 5.9	−10.4	−19.8	+10.1	− 8.5
Urban structure	+30.8	+13.6	+18.1	+ 8.6	+10.6	− 2.2	+ 8.1	+ 3.9	+14.7	−18.9	+ 3.8
Size structure	+ 1.2	− 2.4	+ 0.1	− 4.3	+ 2.4	− 1.6	− 0.6	+ 1.5	+ 1.2	+ 1.2	− 0.3
Regional policy	− 1.8	+15.1	+ 3.2	+14.1	− 3.4	− 3.6	+ 6.5	− 1.1	+11.9	− 5.0	+ 0.5
(Residual)	+ 6.6	− 5.3	+ 1.4	− 0.8	+ 4.6	+ 1.7	−10.2	+ 3.7	−11.9	+ 6.1	− 4.0
Net change	+28.6	+ 9.5	+ 7.4	+ 2.5	+ 0.4	−13.0	−14.1	−14.4	−15.9	−18.5	−20.5

Methods of estimation are described in Appendix C.

make, the accounts provide a reasonable guide to the main cause of growth and decline in each region.

Several important conclusions emerge from the employment accounts. Firstly, national decline is an important influence on all regions and, even though some regions manage to stay well above the average, the pervasiveness of national decline is sufficient to produce a strong downward bias in regional manufacturing employment change. Thus only one region, East Anglia, increased its employment by more than ten per cent, while six regions lost more than ten per cent. Secondly, divergences from the national rate of employment change are really only the net result of conflicting influences on growth. There is no region in which all four causes of uneven growth worked in the same direction between 1960 and 1975. For example, Yorkshire and Humberside lost only slightly more employment than the national average, but this hides a heavy loss of jobs due to an adverse industrial structure, a smaller loss due to regional policy, and gains because of the urban-rural shift and an above-average proportion of employment in smaller plants.

Thirdly, the four causes of uneven growth vary in magnitude across the country as a whole, as well as within individual regions. Urban structure has been the most powerful influence on the pattern of change, reflecting the marked differences in the extent to which each region's industry is concentrated in cities, towns or rural areas. The role of industrial structure has been more variable: in one or two regions its impact has been substantial, but elsewhere it had a more modest influence. Regional policy, too, has been important in the three smaller development area regions—Wales, Northern Ireland and the North—but not so much elsewhere. Size structure has been the least important of the four factors at this regional scale, principally because some of the sharper contrasts between individual towns are hidden when the towns are aggregated into regions. In the future, of course, the balance between the four influences on growth is likely to be rather different because, as we have shown, the role of both industrial structure and regional policy has diminished in recent years.

The 'residual'
The combined influence of the four factors accounts for most of the regional variation in manufacturing employment change, but does not sum exactly to the actual employment change in each region during these years. There is a residual unexplained element in each region which is small in most but somewhat larger in Scotland and Northern Ireland. At least part of this unexplained portion of

employment change reflects minor influences on growth that are specific to individual regions, the most important of which is the loss of jobs in Northern Ireland due to the political violence in the 1970s. In the 1960s Northern Ireland's manufacturing employment grew faster than in the U.K. as a whole, but in the early 1970s this trend was reversed quite sharply. If we assume that the different shift (the change after allowing for industrial structure) into Northern Ireland would have slowed anyway because of the lessening impact of regional policy, but only by as much as in the other development area regions, then by 1979 a loss of 20–25,000 jobs can be attributed to the troubles. This loss is sufficiently large to account for the whole of the remaining unexplained portion of employment change in this region.

However, specific factors such as Northern Ireland's troubles seem unlikely to account for all the unexplained portion of change in Table 8.1, particularly as the residuals display a distinctive centre-periphery pattern: the southern and midland regions all fare a little better than we would expect, and the regions of the north and west a little worse. The largest negative residual in Great Britain is also found in the most peripheral region, Scotland. Nevertheless, this apparent centre-periphery contrast probably represents no more than inaccuracies in estimating the employment change associated with two of the four factors.

One of these concerns size structure. As we have explained, the size structure of manufacturing plants in each area is the main influence upon the local rate of job creation in new firms. However, Chapter 6 noted that firms set up by graduates show the fastest average growth in both turnover and employment, and argued that the southern and midland regions, and the South East in particular, probably have a greater proportion of firms founded by such people because a larger proportion of their manufacturing employment is in managerial, technical and professional occupations. If this is the case, the effect would be to boost the employment created by new firms in the southern regions. The advantage conferred on them by a favourable size structure, and thus an above-average rate of new-firm formation, is therefore probably greater than that shown in the employment accounts, though by itself this factor could not explain all their residual advantage over peripheral regions.

The main reason why the residual displays a centre-periphery contrast is undoubtedly the way in which the impact of urban structure has been estimated. We have assumed that the urban-rural shift affects each city, town and rural area to the same extent as the average for its 'type', regardless of where in the country it is located. This assumption is not entirely correct. The urban-rural shift occurs via three mechanisms: through competition between firms in cities and small towns, through transfers of production between existing sites within the same company, and through the movement of jobs out of cities to new locations (as complete transfers or new branch plants). Insofar as the shift occurs through competition there is little reason why firms in small towns in southern England should fare better than their rivals in small towns in the north, and as most large companies already operate in many different parts of the country it is also unlikely that shifts from cities to existing sites elsewhere should disfavour peripheral regions to any great extent. But the same is not true of moves out of cities to *new* locations because so much of this movement, which accounts for a quarter to a third of the urban-rural shift, has been out of *London*. Since a disproportionate share of jobs in moves tends to be over short distances, a great many of these jobs stay in southen England. In the 1950s for example, nearly 80 per cent of the employment in moves out of London stayed in the South East, and even after the intensification of regional policy roughly 40 per cent remained in this region. The consequence is that the urban-rural shift benefits small towns in the south and midlands more than small towns in peripheral regions, and though it is not possible to measure this effect very accurately, the pattern and magnitude of the residual in the employment accounts seem broadly in line with what might be expected as a result. So rather than indicating any handicaps to the performance of firms in peripheral regions, the slower growth in these places indicated by the residual probably reflects little more than their remoteness from London.

Employment Change in Two Regions:
The East and West Midlands

The most important conclusion to emerge from the employment accounts nevertheless has nothing to do with centre-periphery contrasts. The accounts demonstrate very clearly that the largest part of regional differences in manufacturing growth can be explained by the four factors we have described in this book. To illustrate this point it is worth comparing two regions, the East and West Midlands.

In many people's minds the English Midlands are grey and undifferentiated; the division into the East and West Midlands is viewed as an administrative convenience rather than an economic, social or physical reality. To some extent this view is justified, because in practice the Midlands comprise a series of city-regions rather than two cohesive functional units. In this sense the Midlands differ from South East England for example, which is dominated by London. The apparent similarity between the two Midland regions is enhanced by the fact that both have seemed relatively prosperous during the post-war period, with unemployment rates normally a little below the national average, and only very small parts of each region have ever received any government assistance. Yet despite being adjacent regions with much in common, the contrast in employment change is sharp. Between 1960 and 1975 the West Midlands lost over one in eight of its manufacturing jobs while employment in the East Midlands remained more or less unchanged. Traditional theories of urban and regional growth are at a loss to explain how this contrast arises, but the employment accounts in Table 8.1 provide an answer. Let us take each of the four factors in turn:

1. *Industrial structure*

Industrially the two regions are rather different. In the West Midlands motor vehicles, engineering and pottery are the dominant employers. In the East Midlands engineering is also important, but so too are hosiery and footwear. Between 1960 and 1975 the industrial structure in the West Midlands favoured employment growth, mainly because the British motor industry was still fairly buoyant during these years, whereas the East Midlands' mix of industries proved a slight handicap, in particular because of the decline of the footwear industry. On balance, the West Midlands' industrial structure boosted its employment by 6–7 per cent relative to its neighbour. Now that the British motor industry is in deep trouble, the West Midlands cannot of course expect to benefit from such a favourable industrial structure.

2. *Urban structure*

The strongest trend in industrial location during the last two decades has been the shift of employment from cities to small towns and rural areas. This, we argued in Chaper 5, seems to be due mainly to the lack of room for expansion—particularly the expansion of existing premises and sites—facing firms in congested urban areas. The urban-rural shift differentiates the East and West Midlands. The West Midlands is one of Britain's most urban regions, with a high proportion of its manufacturing in the Birmingham conurbation and two further major concentrations in the cities of Coventry and Stoke-on-Trent. By comparison, the East Midlands includes three medium-sized cities, Nottingham, Derby and Leicester, each only a fraction of the size of the Birmingham conurbation, and a higher proportion of its manufacturing is in smaller towns and rural areas. We estimate that the balance of cities, towns and rural areas in the two regions led to 12–13 per cent better growth in the East Midlands between 1960 and 1975. This was more than sufficient to offset the West Midlands' advantageous industrial structure.

3. *Size structure*

We have shown that rates of new-firm formation are higher in areas with a high proportion of their employment in small plants, mainly because small and medium-sized firms provide a much more effective training ground for potential founders of new firms. The East Midlands has a heritage of small and medium-sized firms, but in the West Midlands a much larger share of employment is concentrated in big motor and engineering plants (especially in Coventry). The more favourable size structure in the East Midlands, and the consequent higher rate of new-firm formation, is estimated to have boosted its employment by four per cent, relative to its neighbour, between 1960 and 1975.

4. *Regional policy*

With the minor exceptions of Oswestry in the West Midlands, and a small part of the Notts-Derby coalfied in the East Midlands, neither region has received any regional aid. Both have lost jobs to the assisted areas as a consequence. The losses have occurred partly through industrial movement to the assisted areas, and partly because regional policy has led to a better performance of indigenous industry in the assisted areas relative to the South and the Midlands. In terms of absolute numbers, the job losses from the West Midlands have been greater, but we estimate that in relation to the size of each region the impact in the East and West Midlands is probably not very different, at roughly 3–4 per cent of total manufacturing employment.

The combined influence of these four factors explains why the East Midlands has fared so much better than the West Midlands, even though both regions are part of the 'prosperous' non-assisted half of Britain. The East Midlands' less advantageous industrial structure has been more than offset by the better growth resulting from its higher rate of new-firm formation, and by the urban-rural shift in manufacturing location. That it is possible to understand the difference between these two regions—or between other regions for that matter—without reference to traditional theories of industrial location must cast the gravest doubt upon the validity of those theories as explanations for regional growth and decline.

Employment Change in Two Counties: Cleveland and Leicestershire

Our four factors seem able to account for the regional pattern of growth and decline in manufacturing, but regions tend to be large heterogeneous units, and the differences between them in terms of such things as mix of industries, industrial and trade union traditions, and the level of prosperity, are rarely as marked as those between smaller areas. Therefore if our explanation of growth and decline is to be convincing it must also adequately explain the differences and similarities between individual towns and cities with more sharply contrasting industrial and economic environments. The two counties we have chosen to look at more closely are Cleveland and Leicestershire. Partly the choice is pragmatic, because good quality firm-by-firm information exists for both areas, but it is hard to find two counties which, superficially at least, show greater contrasts.

Cleveland, on the north east coast of England, is a product of nineteenth-century industrialisation. The rapid development of the steel industry after 1850 transformed a few hamlets on the banks of the Tees into an industrial sprawl which now embraces Middlesbrough, Stockton, Billingham, Redcar and Hartlepool. In the first half of the twentieth century another major industry developed, chemicals, but despite attempts made since then to diversify the area's industrial structure, steel and chemicals still dominate. As Table 8.2 shows, in 1965 (the beginning of the period at which we shall be looking) roughly 60 per cent of all the area's manufacturing jobs were in these two industries. Moreover, Cleveland is dominated not only by two industries, but by two firms, British Steel and ICI, which still account for over 20,000 jobs each. Even outside these two sectors employment is dominated by a few large employers, and biased towards the 'heavy' end of the spectrum in engineering, for example. In the mid-1960s, no less than four out of five manufacturing jobs were in plants employing 500 or more. Cleveland's fall from prosperity has also been every bit as fast as its initial rise: throughout the post-war period it has been an assisted area, and its unemployment rate is now one of the highest in the country.

Leicestershire, in the heart of the English Midlands, has a much

Table 8.2   Employment by industry in Cleveland and Leicestershire 1965

1965 manufacturing employment	Cleveland 114,500 %	Leicestershire 170,800 %
Food, drink, tobacco	4	5
Chemicals	29	2
Metal manufacture	32	1
Engineering	20	35
Shipbuilding	4	0
Textiles and clothing	6	44
Other	5	13
	100	100
% of employment in plants employing 500+	80	36[1]

[1] 1968.

longer industrial history. Leicester itself (which contains about two-thirds of the county's jobs) has been an important commercial and administrative centre for centuries, and its industrial growth has proceeded more gradually than Cleveland's. Hosiery and footwear are the two traditional employers, though the latter has now declined, but a wide range of other industries, particularly in different branches of engineering, have emerged in the twentieth century to diversify the county's industrial base. Table 8.2 shows that Leicestershire's industrial structure is very different from Cleveland's, and a much smaller proportion of employment is in large plants. A large share of industry is locally owned and controlled—which often prompts the claim that Leicester has more millionaires per head than any other city in Britain—and there is a tradition of weak trade unions and a quiescent labour force. Furthermore, while in Cleveland unemployment has been a perennial problem, in Leicestershire the rate has almost always been below the national average. Industries may come and go, the economy may rise or fall, but somehow Leicestershire never seems to catch a cold.

Employment accounts
To a large extent Cleveland fits every southerner's image of the dirty depressed North, while Leicestershire lives up to the South's reputation for cosy prosperity, yet the same explanation of growth and decline can be applied to both these contrasting areas. To illustrate this point Table 8.3 presents employment accounts for both counties for the period from 1965 to 1976. The methods used to

Table 8.3 Employment accounts for manufacturing: Cleveland and Leicestershire 1965–76

| | Cleveland | | Leicestershire | |
	employees	%	employees	%
1965 employment	114,500	100.0	170,800	100.0
National change	−17,600	−15.4	−26,300	−15.4
Difference due to:				
Industrial structure	− 1,300	− 1.1	− 2,000	− 1.2
Urban structure	+ 3,200	+ 2.8	+ 9,400	+ 5.5
Size structure	− 7,400	− 6.6	+ 6,300	+ 3.7
Regional policy	+11,500	+10.0	− 4,200	− 2.5
(Residual)	+ 300	+ 0.3	+ 2,900	+ 1.7
Net change	−11,300	− 9.9	−13,900	− 8.1

Methods of estimation are described in Appendix C.

derive the accounts are broadly similar to those used to produce the accounts for regions, and are described in Appendix C. Once again attention is drawn to the importance of national economic problems: between 1965 and 1976 manufacturing employment in Cleveland and Leicestershire fell, and in both counties the main factor contributing to this decline was simply the fall in manufacturing employment in the country as a whole. But the interesting feature of Table 8.3 is that manufacturing employment fell at much the same rate in both Cleveland and Leicestershire despite the superficial contrasts between the two areas and despite the massive aid which Cleveland received during these years of intensive regional policy. The factors which brought about this similarity in overall employment change nevertheless differ considerably.

The two counties experienced a similar small loss of jobs due to an adverse industrial structure, which is perhaps surprising given the different combination of industries in each area. This confirms what we have noted previously—that since the mid-1960s industrial structure has generated relatively few disparities in employment change—and also shows that a predominance of heavy industries, such as steel and chemicals, does not necessarily mean that an area like Cleveland has a markedly unfavourable industrial structure. Cleveland and Leicestershire are also similar in that they are both dominated by what we have called free standing cities. In the country as a whole free standing cities are not losing manufacturing jobs as quickly as the conurbations, and have actually fared rather better than the national average, so we estimate that both counties have gained from the urban-rural shift in manufacturing location. But as we know, a large part of Cleveland's employment is in steel and heavy chemicals, two industries which normally operate outside the main built-up areas and consequently do not experience the problem of constrained premises and sites which dogs the rest of industry in cities and large towns. Assuming therefore that steel and heavy chemicals do not display urban-rural contrasts in growth, we estimate that Cleveland, with half its manufacturing jobs in these industries, has gained from the urban-rural shift to only half the extent to which Leicestershire has gained.

Size structure and regional policy have had markedly different impacts upon the two counties. Regional policy has been responsible for a large number of jobs moving into Cleveland, but to a great extent this gain has been offset by the dominance of very large manufacturing plants in the county, leading to a low rate of job creation in new firms. Conversely, in Leicestershire the loss of jobs due to regional policy has been offset by a high rate of job creation in new firms resulting from a favourable size structure.

In both counties the contribution of new firms is based on hard evidence. Our establishment-based data for Leicestershire allows us to measure both the employmemt in firms set up during the period and the net growth of young firms set up during the previous twenty years (which together make up the total 'new firms' effect). In Cleveland, employment in firms set up during the period can also be measured directly using the establishment-based data collected by Robinson and Storey, and the growth of young firms has been estimated on the basis of trends in Leicestershire. The disparity in growth due to new firms—no less than 10 per cent between 1965 and 1976—must therefore be regarded very seriously indeed. On the basis of this evidence there can be little doubt that Leicestershire's higher rate of new-firm formation lies at the root of its greater long-run prosperity. In order to keep up with Leicestershire, Cleveland must remain hooked on injections of new industry from outside. In the recent past the operation of an intensive regional policy has made sure that Cleveland received this injection, but now that policy is being weakened and the supply of mobile branch plants has dried up, the outlook for the county can only be described as grim. Nevertheless, it is worth stressing that the disparity in new-firm formation has nothing to do with the outlook or aspirations of the people living in the two counties. As was shown in Chapter 6, the low rate of formation in 'large plant towns' such as Cleveland occurs because they lack a heritage of small firms to provide a training ground for potential founders of new firms.

There are therefore sharp difference in the causes of growth and decline in Cleveland and Leicestershire. Nevertheless, the four factors which have been emphasised throughout—industrial structure, urban structure, size structure and regional policy—collectively offer an adequate explanation of the levels of employment change in these two very different counties, and in both cases the 'unexplained' portion of employment change is small.

Openings, closures and survivors
The explanation being offered for manufacturing growth extends beyond levels of net employment-change because it also enables us to understand differences in the components of change—the opening, growth and closure of establishments—between the two counties. As Table 8.4 shows, Cleveland is characterised not only by a lower rate of job creation in new firms and higher employment in moves in, but rates of expansion among existing establishments in the county are also lower, rates of contraction are higher, and closures are only half as important as in Leicestershire.

Table 8.4 *The components of manufacturing employment change: Cleveland and Leicestershire*

	Openings			Survivors			
				as % of base year manufacturing employment			
	New firms	Local branches	Moves in	Expansion	Contraction	Closures[1]	Net change
Cleveland 1965–76	+1.6	+1.8	+10.0	+6.8	−21.4	− 8.7	−9.9
Leicestershire 1968–75	+5.7	+4.6	+ 0.6	+17.0	−15.2	−15.3	−2.6

[1] includes transfers out.
Source: Cleveland from Robinson and Storey (1981).

What we are observing in the balance between expansions, contractions and closures is the growth of young firms and the effect of plant size. We showed earlier that young firms, which are mostly quite small, experience high rates of closure, but if they survive are likely to grow quite quickly, even up to twenty years after they were first set up. On the other hand older firms are a source of job losses, and if these old firms are also large firms they tend to lose jobs through contraction rather than complete closure. Leicestershire has a high rate of new-firm formation, so at any time a sizeable proportion of its stock of firms are relatively young, small firms. Consequently job losses in closures tend to be quite high, but the balance between expansions and contractions among surviving firms is favourable. Cleveland shows the opposite characteristics. It is dominated by big long-established companies, and even most of the new branch plants which have been injected into its economy over the years are quite large. Therefore the area experiences a more adverse balance between expansions and contractions, but a relatively low loss of jobs in closures. If Cleveland had a higher rate of new-firm formation—and hence a larger number of young firms emerging to offset the contraction among its larger employers—the picture would not, of course, look so bad.

That there is nothing unusual about the components of change in Cleveland or Leicestershire can also be demonstrated numerically. In Table 8.5 we have calculated 'predicted' rates of growth and closure in each county, based on the size structure of their manufacturing plants and average rates of growth and closure in different sizes of establishment in the East Midlands. By standardis-

Table 8.5   *The influence of plant size on rates of growth and closure in Cleveland and Leicestershire*

		% change in manufacturing employment	
		Closures	Net growth of survivors
Cleveland	Actual	− 8.7	−14.6
1965−76	Predicted[1]	− 8.2	−12.5
Leicestershire	Actual	−15.3	+ 1.8
1968−75	Predicted[1]	−14.1	+ 3.3

[1] on the basis of average annual rates in 7 size bands in the East Midlands between 1968 and 1975 and the size structure of manufacturing plants in each county at the start of the period.

ing for size we are also standardising for the age of firms, because the better net growth of small firms is almost entirely due to young firms, as we showed in Chapter 6. The rates of growth and closure in both counties can thus be predicted very accurately and the conclusion is clear. The different balance between the rates of growth and closure in Cleveland and in Leicestershire reflects no more than the balance between larger, old firms and younger, small firms in the two counties. The actual rates of growth and closure are slightly worse than predicted in both areas, but this too is what we would expect because Cleveland and Leicestershire are dominated by free standing cities, whereas the predicted rates have been calculated using the average rates from the East Midlands, where a great deal of industry is in smaller towns and rural areas. Just as it is possible to identify the *causes* of employment change in Cleveland and Leicestershire, so it is possible to explain the *ways* in which that change has occurred.

A Structural Explanation

In our discussion so far, we have presented a great deal of evidence about the causes of unequal growth in manufacturing employment. At this stage, it might be useful to stand aside from the statistics and look in more general terms at the nature of the explanation we are putting forward. The essence of our explanation is, of course, that the underlying causes of unequal growth are *structural*. All areas have an established manufacturing sector inherited from the past which to varying degrees confers handicaps or benefits upon their subsequent employment growth. We have demonstrated the importance of three inherited structural characteristics—industrial structure, urban structure and size structure. Their individual importance varies to some extent as the fortunes of the national economy rise and fall, but collectively they exert a pervasive influence on the urban and regional pattern of employment change, extending over very long periods. The fourth factor moulding the pattern of change, regional policy, represents the attempt by governments to offset some of the worst inequalities in growth generated by the structural characteristics of different areas. But regional policy can only improve the situation very slowly. The structural problems which face some areas tend to be self-perpetuating and do not correct themselves, so at best regional policy can only transform the position of depressed industrial areas if pursued vigorously over many decades. In advancing this explanation for unequal growth in manufacturing we are at the same time rejecting two popular but misleading explanations.

Firstly, urban and regional differences in employment change have little to do with the qualities of the people living in different areas. Our evidence demonstrates that growth and decline can be understood without introducing any consideration of attitudes to hard work and entrepreneurship, or labour militancy. If cultural factors play some residual role (and this has never been proved) it must be a minor one. The problem of declining employment in Clydeside and Tyneside, for example, cannot be blamed on the local workforce. These two areas, which have experienced some of the worst and most persistent manufacturing decline in the country, are handicapped by all three structural problems. Their mix of shipbuilding and heavy engineering industries does not favour employment growth. As conurbations they find it difficult to provide the room which modern industry requires to expand its sites and premises. And both areas lack the heritage of smaller firms which elsewhere provide the vital training ground for the founders of new firms.

Secondly, the neo-classical location theories of grography and economics are inadequate as descriptions of reality. Their central concern is the interaction between profit-maximising firms and an environment in which costs of production and distribution (and transport costs in particular) vary from place to place, and they postulate that growth will be greatest where firms can minimise their costs and maximise their revenue. These theories do not fit the evidence very well. They ignore the way in which trends in the national economy affect areas differently because of their different mix of industries, and do not accommodate the role of large plants in inhibiting new-firm formation. The location of most new firms has nothing to do with marginal cost and revenue curves—contrary to what neo-classical theories suggest—but instead depends a great deal upon where the founders happen to be living at the time. Moreover, though higher costs may play some part in bringing about one of the structural shifts in employment— from urban to rural areas—our evidence suggests that the lack of room for expansion has been the main cause of the decline of manufacturing in large urban areas.

We must also be explicit on one further point: we are putting forward four factors as an explanation not just for one part of the location of growth and decline, but as the key to understanding the *overall* pattern of unequal growth in manufacturing. Our explanation is not intended to exclude entirely more minor factors. Clearly there are several smaller influences on growth and decline, some of them specific to certain areas, as we have already acknowledged in this chapter. But if any other factor is of major importance then it must be demonstrated how that factor is hidden in the 'unexplained residual' in the employment accounts, or how the disaggregation of employment change we have adopted is fundamentally incorrect. The fact remains that the four factors we have identified satisfactorily account for the largest part of the observed variation in manufacturing employment change.

9 Prospects, Problems and Policies

Chapters 3–8 described the factors which determine the pattern of employment change, how they vary in strength and direction from place to place and from time to time, and how they work together in a complex fashion to bring about unequal growth. These analyses are useful not simply because they provide insights into recent trends but also because they can form the basis of a realistic assessment of future trends in industrial location and employment change. In this final chapter we therefore look briefly at what these trends are likely to be, at the extent to which they will exacerbate existing inequalities in employment opportunities between different parts of the country, and at the viability of alternative policies to reduce those inequalities.

Future Employment Trends

In assessing future urban and regional employment change it is important to make explicit our assumption about the likely trend in the economy as a whole. There are two reasons for this. Firstly, though this book has been mainly concerned with differences between areas, the performance of the national economy has a profound effect on the *level* of employment in every area. Secondly, the growth of the national economy affects the *location* as well as the overall level of employment change. The relative importance of each of the factors which determine the pattern of unequal growth varies as the fortunes of the national economy rise and fall, and insofar as national economic conditions in future years are different from those during much of the post-war period we can therefore expect to observe a rather different pattern of urban and regional change.

Our regional forecasts are based on the assumption that national trends in employment during the 1970s will continue in the 1980s. In other words, total U.K. employment will be roughly the same in 1990 as at the start of the decade, but within this total manufacturing will decline substantially while services will provide an offsetting increase in employment. Given that the labour force will rise relatively quickly during the 1980s, this assumption of stability in total employment implies that unemployment will be roughly 2.75

million in 1990. Since unemployment has been forecast to rise as high as 4.4 million by 1985 if present economic policies are continued (Cambridge Economic Policy Group 1980a), these assumptions about national trends anticipate, by implication, a drastic alteration of economic policy during the 1980s leading to a recovery in employment. Because the alternative—six or seven million unemployed—is unthinkable, a radical change in policy is almost inevitable. But the main point which needs to be made is that our forecasts of future levels of urban and regional employment are *conditional*. They should not be viewed as a prediction of what will happen to national employment, but more as a description of the most likely regional pattern of growth and decline if the adverse national employment trends during the 1970s continue at much the same rate during the 1980s. Having said this however, it is difficult to think of a more plausible assumption about national trends.

It is appropriate to start by considering manufacturing because this sector plays the leading role in determining the overall pattern of employment change. In contrast, primary employment has shrunk to such an extent that it has ceased to exert a major influence on the overall pattern of change, and the largest part of the service sector also exerts little independent influence because so many service jobs follow the location of jobs in other sectors. Within manufacturing, unequal growth is due largely to our four factors— industrial structure, urban structure, size structure and regional policy. At least two of these are likely to be unimportant in a depressed economy.

One is industrial structure. As the national decline has worsened since the mid-1960s, industrial structure has generated fewer and fewer disparities. There has been some convergence in the mix of industries in each region, but the main reason for the demise of industrial structure is that there are no longer large contrasts in employment trends between 'growing' and 'declining' industries. Instead, the decline in employment now affects nearly every branch of manufacturing industry, so while from time to time some regions are hit harder than others because of their reliance on an industry which is suffering particularly severely, as a general rule no region is likely to be greatly advantaged or disadvantaged by its mix of industries. Between 1973 and 1979 most southern and midland regions benefited from a slightly favourable structure, and the peripheral regions from a slightly unfavourable one, though not to any great extent in either case. The most plausible assumption for the 1980s is that these modest rates of structural growth and decline will continue.

Regional policy is the other factor that is likely to be unimportant in a depressed economy. This was moderately successful up to about 1973, largely because a relatively buoyant manufacturing sector generated employment and investment in new branch plants which could be diverted to the assisted areas. The subsequent decline in manufacturing has severely curtailed potentially mobile investment of this sort, and even the limited investment in new factories which has occurred in assisted areas has invariably been so capital intensive that it has provided few jobs. Not surprisingly, there is evidence that regional policy had hardly any impact in the second half of the 1970s. So long as manufacturing continues to decline there is little hope for a resumption in the supply of jobs in new branch plants, and it is therefore unlikely that traditional regional policies will have much effect in the 1980s.

The two other causes advanced for the unequal growth in manufacturing—urban structure and size structure—are likely to alter in ways which will make future trends different to those of the recent past. Urban structure will remain the more important of the two although its importance is likely to diminish. In Chapter 5 we argued that the main reason why manufacturing employment is declining in the cities is the inadequacy of industrial sites and premises, compared with smaller towns and rural areas. In urban factories with no room for expansion investment in new machinery displaces labour on the shop floor, leading to falling employment, and new factory floorspace is located mainly in small towns and rural areas where it can more easily be accommodated. The shortage of space in cities is unlikely to disappear, even though urban authorities are now adopting more sympathetic attitudes towards industry. However, in the period of slower growth now facing the British economy the lack of room for expansion will in any case be less of a constraint than in the past, with the result that the relative decline of the cities will slow down to perhaps half the average rate of the 1960s and early 1970s. The remaining shifts in employment are nevertheless likely to be large. If the urban-rural shift slows by half, London alone will still lose another 100,000 manufacturing jobs by the end of the decade, over and above its share of any national contraction in manufacturing employment.

Service employment is not decentralising as quickly, and some service activities may even be drifting in the opposite direction, so the urban-rural shift in total employment will not be as dramatic as in manufacturing alone. Indeed, looking ahead to the end of the century, a remarkable transformation which began in earnest around 1960 may be nearing completion. To a large extent Britain's cities will have reverted to their traditional medieval role as service centres for their hinterlands, the difference this time being that they will serve hinterlands which are primarily industrial, not agricultural. The 'industrial city', which grew up in the nineteenth and early twentieth centuries, is proving a transient phenomenon.

Towns dominated by small and medium-sized companies will continue to benefit from above-average rates of new-firm formation. There is evidence that rates of formation rose during the 1970s, and also that more new firms are set up in periods of high unemployment, so it is likely that the rate of formation will be higher in coming years than during much of the post-war period, irrespective of current attempts to increase the number of new firms. In forecasting the location of manufacturing employment change we have assumed that in the 1980s the disparities attributable to new firms, between large and small plant areas, will be half as great again as those we observed during the 1960s and early 1970s.

Future trends in the location of manufacturing jobs will therefore probably have more in common with the late 1970s than with earlier periods. Unlike the 1950s industrial structure will not help or hinder any region to a significant extent, and unlike the 1960s regional policies will probably provide few jobs in assisted areas. Large cities, especially those dominated by large firms, such as Glasgow, Liverpool and Coventry, will decline the most, while less-urbanised small plant areas will suffer less de-industrialisation. If we assume that national manufacturing employment falls by 20 per cent between 1980 and 1990—much the same decline as during the 1970s—these trends lead to the predictions of manufacturing employment change shown in Table 9.1.

Table 9.1   Projected changes in manufacturing employment by region 1980–90

	Change	as % 1980 manufacturing employment
East Anglia	− 15,000	− 8.0
South West	− 55,000	−13.0
East Midlands	− 85,000	−15.0
Yorkshire and Humberside	− 120,000	−18.0
South East	− 330,000	−19.0
West Midlands	− 200,000	−22.0
North West	− 205.000	−22.0
North	− 95,000	−24.0
Wales	− 65,000	−24.0
Scotland	− 145,000	−26.0
Northern Ireland	− 35,000	−27.0
U.K.	−1,350,000	−20.0

Forecasts to 1990

In East Anglia, the South West and East Midlands, manufacturing will probably decline much less than in the country as a whole, mainly because the slower but continuing urban-rural shift will benefit these regions, as it has done during the last two decades. In the South East and Yorkshire and Humberside the decline is also likely to be less than in the U.K. as a whole, but only marginally. Though the anticipated loss of jobs in the South East remains large this represents an improvement in the region's trend relative to the national average, which was particularly unfavourable in the 1960s and the first half of the 1970s. The improvement results partly from the slower rate at which London will decline, in line with the probable slowing in the overall urban-rural shift, and partly because the reduced effectiveness of regional policy will mean that the South East will lose fewer jobs to the assisted areas. The decline of London will nevertheless ensure that manufacturing employment continues to fall faster in the South East than in neighbouring, less urbanised, regions. Yorkshire and Humberside has never relied heavily on regional policy to provide an inflow of jobs, so the diminishing impact of policy will not matter here, and underlying trends in the region have always been better than in the North West or Scotland for example, so we anticipate that manufacturing employment will not fall as rapidly in Yorkshire and Humberside as in other northern regions.

In the remaining regions—Scotland, Wales, Northern Ireland, the West Midlands, the North and the North West—manufacturing employment is projected to fall faster than the national average. This represents a serious deterioration in Wales and the North in particular, where manufacturing growth was well above average in the 1960s and 1970s. The deterioration mainly reflects the smaller impact which traditional regional policies are likely to make, and the failure of policy will mean that Scotland's performance also stays below average. Employment change in Northern Ireland depends a great deal upon the province's political problems. We have assumed that they will lead to perhaps only half the job losses associated with the troubles in the 1970s (which we estimated at 20–25,000 jobs), but such losses will still be sufficient to keep the province at the bottom of the growth league. The West Midlands and North West are both dominated by conurbations, and will therefore continue to be handicapped by the urban-rural shift in industrial location. Over and above these factors, the peripheral location of all but the West Midlands among this group of rapidly declining regions will mean that their smaller towns will not benefit from the urban-rural shift to quite the same extent as in other parts of the country.

The conditional nature of these forecasts must be stressed. If the national decline in manufacturing employment is larger or smaller than we have assumed, the change in every region will be larger or smaller than the figures put forward, but unless there is a reversal of long-term national economic trends, or a revival of regional policy—both of which seem unlikely at the present time—the ordering of the regions will probably differ little from the one we have described. Also, because these forecasts are grounded in an analysis of the factors which determine regional employment change, and how the importance of those factors changes through time, they are likely to be significantly more accurate than a simple straight-line extrapolation of historical trends.

Manufacturing is bearing the brunt of the difficulties faced by the British economy. Employment in other sectors, mostly in services, has actually risen in recent years, and in the 1970s this growth was sufficient to offset manufacturing job losses and keep total U.K. employment more or less unchanged over the decade as a whole. However, as Chapter 3 demonstrated, for every basic job (in the primary or manufacturing sectors) gained or lost relative to the country as a whole, a region could in the long run expect to gain or lose a further job in the service sector, so the expansion in service employment was far from evenly spread. This close relationship between the location of manufacturing and service jobs is important because it enables our estimates of likely changes in manufacturing employment to form the basis for predictions of total employment change in each region between 1980 and 1990. Five additional assumptions are necessary:

1. Primary employment will remain unchanged in total (the steep decline in primary employment has come to an end in recent years).
2. Employment in construction and public utilities will fall at the same rate as between 1970 and 1980.
3. Employment in private sector services will grow at the same rate as between 1970 and 1980.
4. Employment in public sector services will grow at half the rate between 1970 and 1980.
5. The same one-for-one multiplier from basic employment to service employment will continue in each region.

Taken together these assumptions imply that total U.K. employment will remain unchanged—much the same overall trend as in the 1970s, as we have already noted. The estimates of total employment change, disaggregated by region, are shown in Table 9.2. The expansion in services will prop up employment everywhere, offsetting some of the manufacturing decline, but, because so much

Table 9.2 *Projected employment shortfalls by region 1980–90*

	as % 1980 labour force			Employment shortfall 1980–90[2]		Unemployment 1990[2]
	Unemployment June 1980	Employment change 1980–90	Increase in labour supply[1]	Number	% 1980 labour force	
Northern Ireland	12.7	−2.5	14.5	100,000	17.0	18.2
West Midlands	6.8	−5.0	6.5	265,000	11.5	11.8
Scotland	9.9	−2.5	7.5	225,000	10.0	14.7
North	10.3	−3.0	5.5	115,000	8.5	15.0
North West	8.8	−3.0	4.5	215,000	7.5	13.4
Yorkshire & Humberside	7.2	0	6.5	135,000	6.5	11.7
Wales	9.1	−1.5	5.0	70,000	6.5	13.6
East Midlands	6.2	+1.5	6.5	80,000	5.0	10.5
South East	4.3	+2.5	4.5	150,000	2.0	8.3
South West	6.1	+4.5	5.0	10,000	0.5	10.0
East Anglia	5.2	+7.5	6.5	(− 5,000)	(−1.0)	8.9
U.K.	6.9	0	5.6	1,360,000	5.6	11.3[3]

[1] percentage change in population of working age due to natural increase (estimated by cohort survival), plus a 2.0 per cent increase in labour supply attributable to rising activity rates.
[2] increase in labour supply minus increase in employment 1980–90.
[3] assumes net emigration equal to 1.2 per cent of 1980 labour force.

service employment follows manufacturing, the regional pattern of change in total employment will be broadly similar to that for manufacturing alone. The main differences involve the South East, where a low proportion of employment in manufacturing favours total employment growth, and the East and West Midlands, where a high proportion in manufacturing will depress overall employment change.

Employment Shortfalls

The pattern of regional employment change is important because of its social implications. Table 9.2 shows the estimated change in the labour supply in each region arising from the natural increase in the workforce and from the steady rise in activity rates as more women seek employment. Together with the projected employment changes, the rise in the labour supply allows us to calculate the *employment shortfall* in each region. This is the difference between the increase in the number of people seeking work and the change in employment between 1980 and 1990. It provides the best indicator of employment problems in each region because, by definition, an employment shortfall must lead either to additional unemployment (registered or unregistered) or to out-migration, or a combination of both.

The shortfall in the country as a whole resulting from the assumed stagnation in total employment will ensure that in most regions the supply of labour rises faster than the supply of jobs. The severity of the shortfall is likely to vary considerably, however. This is disturbing because the projected shortfalls will exacerbate existing inequalities in employment opportunities rather than reduce them. As Table 9.2 shows, in six out of the seven regions where the employment shortfall during the 1980s is likely to be above average, rates of unemployment are *already* above average, sometimes markedly so. In Northern Ireland, where the rate of unemployment is the highest in the United Kingdom, the shortfall in the 1980s will probably be the largest—equal to about one in six of the workforce. In contrast, in four regions where unemployment is currently below average the likely shortfall will be the smallest, and in one of these, East Anglia, the growth in employment may marginally outstrip the growth of the indigenous labour force. Variations in the projected shortfall are not simply the result of differences in employment change. In Northern Ireland in particular, and Scotland to a lesser extent, the above-average natural increase in the labour force plays an important part in exacerbating the problem. But the important point is that whatever the cause, when the growth in the number of jobs lags behind the growth in the number of people seeking work, the result must be either net out-migration or higher unemployment.

In the past, migration has absorbed much of the imbalance in regional labour markets, so disparities in the growth of unemployment have been much more modest than disparities in employment change. Where the shortfall in employment has been greatest there has been out-migration; where employment has grown faster than the indigenous labour supply there has been in-migration. Indeed migratory flows have been large enough to ensure that rates of unemployment have risen everywhere, even though the growth of employment has been so unequal, because many migrants into the more prosperous regions have taken jobs which would otherwise have gone to local people, who have thus been forced into the dole queue.

Though migration has been substantial it has stopped short of removing inequalities in the growth of unemployment. The experience of 1966–78 (Cambridge Economic Policy Group 1980b) shows that in regions in which the employment shortfall was greater than the national average, the increase in unemployment was also above average. However, the additional increase in unemployment amounted to only 10 per cent of the amount by which the shortfall exceeded the national rise in unemployment, while migratory flows absorbed the remaining 90 per cent. Assuming that this relationship between employment shortfalls and migration continues during the 1980s, it is possible to estimate likely unemployment rates in each region in 1990. These are shown in the last column of Table 9.2 and illustrate the particularly slow response of the pattern of unemployment to changes in employment in each region. It is nevertheless worth emphasising that some of the largest increases in unemployment are likely to occur where unemployment is already well above average.

In the future the role of migration in removing the worst imbalances in regional labour markets may in fact be more limited than during the last ten or fifteen years. The depressed conditions which are likely to prevail will not only cut the number of new jobs on offer in 'prosperous' regions, but also the reduction in labour turnover normally experienced in periods of high unemployment will mean that fewer existing jobs will fall vacant there. The opportunities for leaving a depressed area to move to a job elsewhere will thus diminish, and consequently the inequalities in the growth of unemployment may be greater than those we have anticipated. But in any case, as a great deal of inter-regional migration is undoubtedly forced on people who are unable to find suitable work where they already live, migration ought not to be assumed to be a painless way of avoiding higher unemployment in depressed areas.

Probable trends in regional employment and the resulting shortfalls in job opportunities therefore pose severe problems, but the issues are not quite so clear-cut at the sub-regional scale. Within each region there has been a strong movement of jobs and people out of cities and into small towns, much of which has occurred without causing grave social problems, and at least part of which seems to accord with changing residential preferences. Few people would argue that the decentralisation of jobs and population from large cities is a wholly bad thing, and for many years this shift was actively promoted by planning policies. But in recent years there has been growing evidence that outward movement from the cities is proceeding too quickly: the loss of jobs is creating pockets of high unemployment in inner city areas, which in turn is disturbing their social balance and diverting private investment in the physical fabric into places where it is needed less urgently.

We have argued that the relative decline in employment in Britain's big cities will continue but at a slower rate, as the urban-rural shift in industrial location slows across the whole urban hierarchy. Assuming that some people will prefer to move to smaller towns and rural areas anyway, the slower relative decline of employment in the cities may cause less distress than the rapid decline of the last two decades, and unemployment rates in inner city areas may not rise still further above the national average. But it is extremely unlikely that the urban-rural shift in employment will slow to such an extent that unemployment in inner city areas falls relative to the rest of the country. The inner city problem, which rose to prominence so quickly in the 1970s, is therefore likely to be with us for some years to come.

National Solutions to Local Problems

All major political parties in Britain accept that both inner city problems and long-standing regional disparities should be an important concern of government policy. The consensus that something must be done is not matched however by agreement about the correct approach, or about the vigour with which urban and regional policies need to be pursued.

The crucial point which must be made is that the solution to high unemployment in depressed areas no longer lies with urban and regional policies alone. Quite simply, unemployment is now too high everywhere, and in these circumstances the solution lies instead with national economic policy. The pervasiveness of national decline is something to which we have drawn attention several times. The fall in national manufacturing employment since the mid-1960s, for example, led to slower growth (or faster decline) in every region, and no region has been exempt from the spate of closures which has characterised British industry at the start of the 1980s. The consequence is that Scotland, Wales and the North now suffer from very high unemployment not because the collapse in their economies has been so much more dramatic than elsewhere, but primarily because the national economy is in decline, and in the so-called prosperous regions unemployment rates are also now above those which prevailed in depressed areas in the 1960s. Looking to the future, our forecasts suggest that unless national trends can be reversed this pattern of rising unemployment in all areas is likely to be repeated. Even in those regions where there may be little or no shortfall in employment, the influx of migrants from more hard-pressed parts of the country will push up local unemployment.

So long as high unemployment persists across the country as a whole, the best way to assist depressed regions and inner city areas, and to help the rest of the country at the same time, is by reducing *national* unemployment. Recent experience illustrates this point. Two decades of intensive regional policy succeeded in raising manufacturing employment in the assisted areas by roughly a quarter of a million, but the decline in the national economy during 1980 alone was sufficient to add at least this number of people to the dole queues in the same areas. Moreover, even during the late 1960s, when regional policy was pursued more vigorously than at any other time during the last thirty years and when national economic problems were less acute, the flow of new factories into the assisted areas failed to prevent a substantial rise in unemployment there in line with national trends.

The difficulty in solving regional unemployment in isolation from wider national unemployment problems is compounded by the role of inter-regional migration. As we noted, where employment growth is above average the main result is in-migration from other areas, rather than lower unemployment, and in depressed areas the unemployment figures hide the true magnitude of the problem because so many people are forced to migrate to other parts of the country in search of work. The most important consequence of a successful regional policy is therefore to stem out-migration, while unemployment itself falls only very slowly towards the national average.

A recovery in the national economy, and the large reduction in unemployment it can produce in all areas, must therefore be the overriding priority, though there are inevitably conflicting views about how such a recovery can be achieved. Our own view is expressed by the Cambridge Economic Policy Group (1980a) who argue that the policies pursued in recent years by both Labour and Conservative administrations have been wrong, and that the strategy for recovery must be based on higher investment, expansionary monetary and fiscal policies, and the planned growth of imports within levels which are compatible with full employment. If there is to be a solution to high unemployment in depressed areas this national strategy, we believe, is essential. This is not to say that urban and regional policies are by any means irrelevant. On the contrary, they have an important role to play. A reversal of the decline in the national economy would not by itself bring an end to unequal growth, even though it could benefit all areas. Likewise, as our forecasts indicated, if the adverse national trends of the 1970s are repeated during the 1980s the pattern of employment change will exacerbate inequalities in employment opportunities rather than reduce them. The need for some sort of urban and regional policy therefore persists.

Partial Remedies

Why not persevere with the same sorts of policies that have been tried in the past—a combination of financial inducements in depressed areas and controls on development in more prosperous regions? The most serious objection to this approach is that it is no longer having much success. Although regional policy raised manufacturing employment in the assisted areas during the 1960s and early 1970s, in more recent years traditional methods have had little impact because the conditions for their success, in particular investment in new branch plants, have disappeared as the national economy has deteriorated. At the same time the shortcomings of earlier successes have now become apparent because twenty years of intensive policy have failed to create the basis for self-sustaining growth in the assisted areas. For example, there is no evidence that the manufacturing industrial structures in the development area regions were any more favourable for employment growth in the 1970s than in the early 1950s.

Even if economic conditions were more favourable, traditional regional policies would still be overdue for a major overhaul. For a start, their emphasis on subsidies to capital investment is inappropriate. Following the withdrawal of the Regional Employment Premium, all major forms of regional aid are now geared to capital investment and none to labour, even though the main problem in the assisted areas is high unemployment. The present policies are also wasteful. Capital grants are paid to all manufacturing firms in the assisted areas to cover a fixed percentage of their expenditure on new plant and machinery, an incentive which has the virtue of certainty in that firms know in advance what they will receive, but one which means that many millions are paid to companies for capital intensive projects which create only a few jobs. As many of these schemes would in any case have gone ahead in the assisted areas, the grants may also serve to increase profits or wages, but not employment. It may of course be legitimate from the point of view of national industrial policy to subsidise captial investment even when there is little immediate gain in employment, but such a policy ought not be conducted under the guise of 'helping depressed areas'. A more sensible approach, if the Regional Development Grant is retained, would be to impose a definite ceiling, in terms of cost-per-job, above which further subsidy would be discretionary, not automatic as at present.

One response to the inadequacy of traditional policy, with its emphasis on public spending and intervention, is the resurgence of interest in a more *laissez-faire* approach to urban and regional problems. In particular the present Conservative Government has reduced regional investment grants, turning instead to a reliance on individual enterprise and initiative, and upon the small firm in particular. In practical terms this has led to changes in legislation and taxation designed to encourage small firms, and to the creation of 'enterprise zones' in several depressed areas, where generous tax concessions and exemptions from planning controls are available.

The sorts of measures which could raise rates of new-firm formation are discussed later, but the important point is that current initiatives are unlikely to have much effect, in part at least because they owe more to political ideology than to hard evidence about the real problems facing small firms. International comparisons, for example, do not support the claim that the British small firm sector has been held back by high taxation and bureaucracy. Our East Midlands data, a case in point, shows that on balance single-plant independent firms added just over 2.5 per cent to the region's manufacturing employment between 1968 and 1975 (Fothergill and Gudgin 1979c) whereas figures for the United States (Birch 1979), where attitudes and rates of taxation are supposedly more favourable towards free enterprise, show net *decline* in comparable firms between 1969 and 1976. It is therefore difficult to see what replicating American conditions for enterprise could achieve in

Britain. In addition, there is no evidence that new-firm formation has declined as tax rates have risen during the post-war period.

A very different response to the failings of traditional regional policy is not to encourage enterprise and the free market but to strengthen centralised control over industrial location. These proposals vary from 'planning agreements' between central government and major industrial companies, covering among other things the location of employment, through to extensive nationalisation and direct public control over investment. If a planned economic strategy of this sort is ever pursued its main purpose will no doubt be to achieve national economic objectives, and it must be in those terms in which its value is ultimately assessed. However, a strategy which extends control to cover the full range of locational decisions taken by companies also has obvious advantages in tackling urban and regional problems.

Unfortunately, the potential achievements of a planned approach to urban and regional economic development remain limited in the depressed conditions which now prevail. The problem is not too different from that facing traditional regional policy: it is a lot easier to control the location of new factories than to alter employment in existing ones, and few new factories are currently being built. Planning agreements or nationalisation may provide greater control over employment levels in existing plants, but whether these controls can always be used to much effect is another matter. In many instances where a small addition to employment and production is involved (and most additions are likely to be small in coming years) it is simply not feasible to hive off growth into a new branch plant several hundreds of miles away; nor is it easy to break up existing production units for dispersal to depressed areas. A great deal of industrial production within firms is highly interrelated, and for that reason best kept together under one roof. Furthermore, there will often be compelling reasons—such as the age of plant and machinery—why if closures are necessary within a multi-plant firm some may have to occur in areas where unemployment is already high. Any approach to regional policy which ignores these realities may provide jobs where they are needed, but only at the expense of industrial efficiency.

Tackling the Problem
So far we have painted a gloomy picture of the opportunities for solving urban and regional problems. Traditional regional policies have met with only limited success, especially in recent years, and the alternatives proposed by both the left and right do not offer a

great deal more. The weakness of the national economy, which is likely to undermine much of the effort to help depressed areas, is part of the reason for this pessimism, but only part. At least as important is the failure of traditional policies and alternatives such as enterprise zones to get to grips with the *causes* of decline in depressed areas. All are designed to offset the decline rather than to alter underlying trends, which is perhaps not surprising given that the factors determining those trends have not been properly understood in the past.

The findings presented in this book indicate two ways in which the underlying causes of unequal growth in manufacturing, the key sector, might be attacked by appropriate policies. The first concerns attempts to slow the urban-rural shift to a rate which creates fewer problems. The main cause of decline in large cities seems to be that too many firms find themselves in constrained locations, operating with inadequate premises and sites, hemmed in by existing urban development, and with no room for expansion. This problem will never be totally overcome because it is inherent in the nature of large cities, but sensitive planning policies could bring an improvement. Tentative steps have already been taken in this direction. Planning authorities now adopt a more sympathetic attitude to the require- ments of industry in urban areas, even where industry does not fit neatly with land-use zoning policies. But this does not go far enough.

A few local authorities have moved closer to what is needed by designating 'industrial improvement areas' within which they assemble sites, reorganise access, construct new factory units and liaise more closely with firms to overcome the physical constraints presented by their existing premises. If the decline of industry in Britain's cities is to be slowed, this approach needs to be pursued vigorously on a city-wide basis, with the aim of removing the obstacles which currently prevent the location of additions to industrial floorspace in major urban areas, both in new factories and in extensions to existing factories. The partial relaxation of greenbelt controls, to allow more factory building on the periphery of urban areas, would assist in achieving this goal.

One effective way to proceed would be to conclude 'local development agreements' between metropolitan local authorities and each major employer within their areas. Under the terms of these agreements the local authority would use its statutory powers to assemble land for employers, particularly land adjacent to their existing factories, in exchange for a commitment on the part of the company to undertake expansion within that locality. Since the lack of room for expansion in urban areas seems in the past to have forced many city-based firms to divert growth into small towns and rural areas, or even to forgo expansion altogether, a commitment to local expansion should not, normally, be difficult to obtain. This approach to slowing urban decline would need to be backed by adequate public funds—to assemble and develop sites, for example. Local authorities would also have to devote sufficient professional and administrative manpower to the task in order to implement schemes which would often be complex—though at least some resources could be released by curbing the New Towns programme outside the assisted areas. Nevertheless, our evidence suggests that this sort of policy would, in the context of urban areas, be more effective than old-fashioned investment incentives. Indeed, policies which induce firms to move into urban areas from elsewhere tackle only a small part of the problem. They do nothing to stem the decline of employment in existing factories in major cities.

The gains from this approach to urban problems are greater than at first appears. The figures we have presented show that though some of the shift of jobs from cities to small towns occurs within companies, much takes place through competition as urban firms in constrained factories either have to forgo expansion or lose business to their competitors. This is important, since some of these competitors are likely to be abroad rather than in small towns and rural areas in Britain. Insofar as the lack of room for physical expansion facing firms in Britain's cities undermines their ability to compete, it therefore poses a problem for the economy as a whole. The potential benefit to the national economy thus provides further justification for a programme of land assembly and factory building in urban areas.

The second way to attack underlying trends in manufacturing employment would be to narrow differences in rates of new-firm formation by increasing the number of entrepreneurs in areas dominated by large plants, where rates of formation are well below average. Current efforts to raise rates of new-firm formation by cutting income tax and 'red tape' are largely misdirected. Our survey of new companies, for example, suggested that most founders are motivated by independence rather than income. Moreover, as has already been noted, there is no apparent relationship between levels of personal taxation and new-firm formation. The main problem holding back new-firm formation in 'large plant towns', and hence in the country as a whole, seems to be that large manufacturing plants fail to provide an adequate training ground for potential founders of new firms. This is reflected in the fact that the employees of existing small firms are many times more likely to start their own business than those working in large firms.

One hopeful possibility for increasing the rate of formation of new firms in depressed areas would therefore be to provide potential founders with relevant experience and training. This might be organised in a number of ways, but would probably include a scheme to allow potential founders to work in small firms to gain the experience necessary to run their own businesses. In the short run new firms do not provide many jobs in any area, so efforts to raise rates of formation in large-plant towns cannot be expected to provide a quick solution to the problem. Moreover, as new firms are usually very small, many thousands of people would need to be involved in such a scheme if it were to have much effect. But as we have shown, in the long run new firms can be a substantial source of jobs, and they can act as an important mechanism through which an area's industrial structure can adapt and diversify. Consequently, a policy to raise rates of new-firm formation, based on training not tax cuts, could form an important element in a strategy to regenerate certain depressed areas, and would complement policies which aim to provide more immediate assistance.

Thus it would seem that there are some neglected and potentially effective measures which could improve the underlying employment trends in depressed areas. How acceptable these measures would be is, of course, a political matter. The use of scarce urban land to provide more room for industry is not popular in all circles, and new small firms have a reputation for paying low wages and failing to observe employment and safety legislation, which does not endear them to everyone. But the costs must be weighed against the benefits.

To conclude, however, we must return to the crucial point made earlier. Britain's industrial base is shrinking so rapidly that any reduction in unemployment which urban and regional policies might achieve in depressed areas is far less than the reduction which a reversal of national trends could produce. The first priority for those in Scotland, South Wales, the North East and elsewhere who are desperately worried by rising unemployment must therefore be to secure a change in *national* economic policy, to halt the destruction of British industry. We believe that the appropriate strategy should be based on reflation backed by the regulation of imports. Reflation is the best way to reduce unemployment in all areas. It also lays the foundation for more effective regional policies because there is little hope that the traditional tools of regional policy will achieve very much in a period of national economic decline. Intensified competition for a dwindling number of mobile branch plants does not confront the main problem now facing depressed areas. Nor can 'special pleading' for more aid in this or that area be expected to achieve a great deal in the absence of an upturn in the national economy.

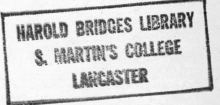

HAROLD BRIDGES LIBRARY
S. MARTIN'S COLLEGE
LANCASTER

Appendix A Data Sources

1. Regional Employment Statistics 1952–79

The figures for employees in employment by region are based upon statistics originally collected by the Department of Employment, and the methods used in the construction of the series have been described fully elsewhere (Fothergill and Gudgin 1978). The figures have been adjusted to be comparable through time by allowing for discontinuities in the original data. These occurred at different times and for different reasons, as follows:

in 1959, because of the introduction of the 1958 Standard Industrial Classification;

in 1964, because of a modification in the methods of compilation;

in 1966, because of the reclassification of many establishments associated with the introduction of Selective Employment Tax;

in 1968, because of the introduction of the 1968 Standard Industrial Classification;

in 1971, because of the change-over from the National Insurance Card Count to the Census of Employment; and

at several points in time to allow for changes in regional boundaries.

Other minor adjustments have been made to specific industries, and for the purpose of deducting unemployed persons, so as to place the figures on a comparable basis, but there are also residual inaccuracies in the original Department of Employment data which are not removed by the adjustment procedures. A full assessment of the reliability of the Department's employment data can be found in Allen and Yuill (1978).

The regions used are those defined for official statistical purposes between 1965 and 1973. The North, Yorkshire and Humberside, the North West, South West, East Midlands and South East differ slightly from the regions as currently defined. All figures have been placed on a basis comparable with the Department of Employment figures on the card count basis and the 1968 Standard Industrial Classification. They are therefore not comparable with the figures currently produced by the Department. In the absence of up-to-date results from the Census of Employment, statistics for 1977–9 are derived from the Department of Employment's quarterly estimates of employees in employment. This has required additional estimation affecting East Anglia, the South East and Northern Ireland in particular.

2. Sub-Regional Employment Statistics 1959–75

These are also based on the statistics originally collected by the Department of Employment, and relate to the 61 sub-regions of Great Britain used for official statistical purposes between 1965 and 1973. The methods used to adjust these figures so that they are comparable through time are broadly similar to those used for the regional statistics, but the two sets of figures are not directly comparable because the sub-regional statistics have been adjusted onto the same basis as the original estimates for 1959. The sub-regional employment figures exclude a very small proportion of employees whose national insurance cards were held at head offices, rather than in the areas in which they were employed, and who were not included in local area statistics. They also include unemployed persons, which introduces a small but unimportant distortion.

3. Industrial Movement 1952–75

The Department of Industry collects statistics on industrial moves, which it defines as transfers plus moves of new branches. To qualify as a move, a new branch must either have an origin (its parent plant) in another sub-region (pre-1966 definition), or must be more than a certain distance from its parent plant (post-1966 definition). Employment figures for moves in and out, by region, are available for certain years:

> for 1945–59 moves, in 1966;
> for 1960–5 moves, in 1966 and 1970;
> for 1966–71 moves, in 1971 and 1975;
> for 1972–5 moves, in 1975.

In some instances it has been necessary to estimate employment in years for which figures are not available (e.g. employment in 1975 in 1960–5 moves). Employment in recent movers is assumed to be building up towards mature levels, and has been estimated using figures for numbers of moves by year and the time profile of employment growth in young branches described in Howard (1968). Mature movers are assumed to show the same net employment change as U.K. manufacturing as a whole, based on the figures from Atkins's (1973) study of employment change 1966–71 in branch plants which moved between 1945 and 1960.

Movement statistics are available for the same areas as the sub-regional employment statistics for 1966–71 moves, with employment in 1971. Figures are available for 1945–65 moves (with employment in 1966) using slightly different sub-regional boundaries, and for 1972–5 moves (with employment in 1975) for counties. In some cases the three sets of boundaries are very similar, but in others employment in moves has been allocated between two or more areas in order to produce estimates for 1952–9 and for 1960–75 on the same boundaries. The build-up of employment has been estimated in the same way as for regions. The figures for employment in moves in or moves out of individual sub-regions are thus subject to greater error than the comparable figures for regions, but many of these errors are self-cancelling where aggregations of sub-regions (e.g. free standing cities, industrial towns) are involved.

The build-up to mature employment levels during 1952–9 of plants which moved to the development area regions between 1945 and 1951 has been estimated using information on numbers of moves per year, 1945–51 into each region and the time profile of build-up to maturity described in Howard (1968). For the purpose of estimating the impact of regional policy, two-thirds of the 1945–51 moves, and two-thirds of the build-up, have been assumed to be policy-induced.

4. Profitability: Mechanical Engineering and Clothing

Financial statistics for companies in these two industries have been published by the National Economic Development Office, for 1969/70 to 1973/4 for clothing (NEDO 1975) and for 1970/1 to 1974/5 for mechanical engineering (NEDO 1976).

The analysis of the information has been restricted to companies operating wholly or mainly within one of the six 'types of area'. The location of companies' factories, including the factories of any subsidiaries, has been identified using addresses supplied by the Business Statistics Office and trade directories. Companies displaying extreme values for profitability are also excluded. Profitability has been measured as the average post-tax rate of profit on capital employed during the five years for which statistics are available for each industry. Table 5.18 expresses profitability in each area as the deviation from the U.K. median profitability for each industry (where industry is defined at sub-MLH level).

5. The East Midlands Industrial Databank

This databank is a unique record containing information on 10,000 individual manufacturing establishments in one region, the East Midlands. The information is based originally on the records of the

Factory Inspectorate (now the Health and Safety Executive), but has been extensively augmented and improved and covers all establishments, including the very smallest, operating in the region in 1968 and 1975. For one part of the region, Leicestershire, the records go back to 1947.

The original information includes the name of each firm, its address, industry and employment at one or more points in time. Details of ownership and control have been identified from *Who Owns Whom* (various years), Who Owns Whom Ltd., London, *Kelly's Manufacturers and Merchants' Directory*, Kelly's Directories Ltd., Kingston Upon Thames, *Industrial Market Location* directories (various years and areas) Industrial Market Location Ltd., Leamington Spa, and listings produced by the Business Statistics Office. The employment in larger establishments has been cross-checked against other data sources.

The records have been organised so that openings, closures, moves and the growth of surviving establishments can each be identified separately. This has necessitated detailed checks using telephone directories and trade directories to establish whether firms have closed or simply moved, and to identify closures not already included in the original Factory Inspectorate lists. Non-manufacturing establishments have been purged from the Factory Inspectorate lists. The coverage has been checked for Leicestershire in 1976, against the directories produced by Industrial Market Location Ltd., which also attempt to achieve a comprehensive coverage of manufacturing establishments, and has been found to be substantially better. A detailed working paper, 'The East Midlands Industrial Databank: a guide to sources, methods and definitions' is available on request from the authors.

6. Annual Rates of New-Firm Formation in the East Midlands

The figures on annual rates of new-firm formation in Figure 6.1 are estimates based on two sample surveys plus information on the total number of post-1947 new firms in the East Midlands which were still operating in 1968 and 1975. The first survey was conducted by post, as described in Gudgin (1978), and identified the date of formation of 127 firms founded after 1940. The second survey, described in Chapter 6, was conducted by interview and provided the date of formation for a further 44 firms set up between 1965 and 1975. The number of firms founded in each year has been revised upwards according to the total number of new firms surviving in 1968 and 1975 included in the East Midlands Industrial Databank.

These estimates of the year of formation of surviving new firms have been further revised to produce estimates of the total number of new firms started in each year, including those which subsequently closed, using a negative exponential survival pattern through time derived for information on all new firms (survivors and closures) in Leicestershire between 1947 and 1957. A similar adjustment to include closures, based upon this pattern of survival through time, has been used to produce the estimates of the number of new firms by period on a comparable basis, shown in the last column of Table 6.4.

Appendix B Classification of Areas

1. Great Britain

The categories are groupings of the 61 sub-regions used for official statistical purposes between 1965 and 1974.

(a) *London*

(b) *Conurbations*
Industrial North East North, West Yorkshire, West Midlands conurbation, Manchester, Merseyside, Glasgow and West Central Scotland.

(c) *Free standing cities*
Industrial North East South, North Humberside, South Yorkshire, Notts-Derby, Leicester, Solent, South West (northern), Coventry, North Staffordshire, Wales (south coast), Edinburgh and East Central Scotland.

(d) *Industrial towns*
Cumberland and Westmorland, South Humberside, Yorkshire coalfield, Northamptonshire, Outer-Metropolitan, West Midlands (central), South Cheshire, South Lancashire, Furness, Mid-Lancashire, North East Lancashire, Central and East Welsh Valleys, West South Wales, North East Wales, Falkirk and Stirling.

(e) *County towns*
Mid-Yorkshire, East Midlands eastern lowlands, East Anglia (south east), East Anglia (north east), East Anglia (north west), East Anglia (south west), Essex, Kent, Sussex Coast, Beds., Berks., Bucks., Oxon., South West (central), South West (southern), Fylde, Lancaster, North Coast Wales, Tayside, North East Scotland.

(f) *Rural areas*
Rural North East North, Rural North East South, South Lindsey, South West (western), West Midlands rural west, North West Wales, Central Wales, South West Wales, Borders, South West Scotland, Highlands and Islands.

2. Great Britain
(Moore, Rhodes and Tyler Classification)

The categories are aggregations of local authority districts. In most instances the boundaries are drawn more tightly around the conurbations and free standing cities than for the sub-regions which form the basis of our own classification (described above), and the allocation of areas to headings differs.

(a) *London*
(b) *Conurbations*
Tyneside, Merseyside, Clydeside, Manchester, West Midlands.
(c) *Free standing cities*
Leeds, Bradford, Sheffield, Nottingham, Leicester, Bristol, Plymouth, Coventry, Stoke on Trent, Edinburgh, Aberdeen, Dundee, Southampton, Portsmouth, Bournemouth and Poole, Brighton and Hove, Cardiff, Hull.
(d) *Hinterlands*
Remainder of Great Britain.

3. East Midlands

The categories are groupings of local authority districts. The definition of the East Midlands region excludes High Peak, Chesterfield, North East Derbyshire, Bolsover, West Lindsey and East Lindsey, but includes Peterborough (from East Anglia).

(a) *Cities*
Nottingham (plus Rushcliffe, Gedling, Broxtowe), Leicester (plus Oadby and Wigston, Blaby), Derby (plus Erewash).
(b) *Larger towns*
Lincoln, Northampton, Peterborough, Mansfield.
(c) *Smaller towns*
Charnwood, Hinckley, Kettering, Wellingborough, Corby, East Northamptonshire, North West Leicestershire, Ashfield, Amber Valley, South Derbyshire, Bassetlaw, Newark.
(d) *Rural areas*
Boston, South Kesteven, South Holland, Melton, Rutland, North Kesteven, Daventry, South Northamptonshire, Harborough, West Derbyshire.

4. European Regions

The grouping of regions in France, West Germany and Italy into 'urban' and 'rural' categories is exceptionally crude because suitable data is not available for smaller units. Hence some of the 'rural' regions also include sizable cities, and the 'urban' regions sometimes include extensive rural hinterlands. The results presented in Table 5.1 should therefore be regarded as only a very broad indicator of employment shifts.

(a) *France*
   Urban regions: Rhone Alpes, Paris, Nord, Provence.
   Rural regions: rest of country.

(b) *West Germany*
   Urban regions: Bremen, Hamburg, West Berlin, Nordheim-Westfalen.
   Rural regions: rest of country.

(c) Italy
   Urban regions: Piedmonte, Lombardia, Lagio, Liguria, Campania.
   Rural regions: rest of country.

Appendix C The Construction of Employment Accounts

1. Employment Accounts for Manufacturing by Region (Table 8.1)

(a) *Net employment change*

The statistics are fully standardised for changes in regional boundaries, methods of compilation and industrial classification (see Appendix A). Pre-1974 regional boundaries are used.

(b) *Industrial structure*

The structural component of a shift-share analysis using 1960 as the base year and disaggregating manufacturing into 99 individual industries.

(c) *Urban structure*

The regional differences due to urban structure are based on the average annual rate of differential shift by type of area between 1959 and 1975, and the share of 1959 manufacturing employment in each type of area in each region. For London and the conurbations the expected shift is based upon a regression line between size and differential shift in these cities. The types of area are defined in Appendix B. Manufacturing employment in Northern Ireland (for which comparable sub-regional data is not available) has been split between the 'free standing city' and 'county towns' categories on the basis of Census of Population data. The differential shift is calculated by a shift-share analysis using 1959 as the base year and disaggregating manufacturing into 99 industries. The steel industry (MLH 311, 312) is excluded from these estimates because it does not normally operate on intra-urban sites and will not therefore experience the constraints associated with urban locations. It has been assumed that there is no urban-rural shift in this industry.

(d) *Size structure*

The size structure of firms in an area leads to disparities in employment change because it influences rates of new-firm formation. In Leicestershire between 1968 and 1975 new firms and young firms (founded 1947–67) together added 1.15 per cent per year to manufacturing employment. Rates of job creation in new and young firms relative to Leicestershire can be estimated using the relationship between rates of new-firm formation and the percentage of employment in plants employing 500 or more (Figure 6.2). The percentage of employment in large plants in each region has been obtained from the Census of Production 1972. A national rate of job creation in new and young firms can also be estimated using these figures, allowing job creation in these firms, and thus disparities due to size structure, to be expressed relative to the national average.

(e) *Regional policy*

The impact of policy on the North, Scotland, Wales and Northern Ireland is estimated for 1960–75 using methods described in Chapter 7. The positive impact of policy on the South West, North West and Yorkshire and Humberside is based upon estimates by Moore, Rhodes and Tyler (1980) for employment in policy-induced moves into these areas. The loss of jobs in other regions arising from regional policy is estimated in three stages:

(i) Two-thirds of the employment in moves to the four development area regions is assumed to be due to policy.

(ii) The employment in policy-induced moves into the South West, North West and Yorkshire and Humberside has been allocated to origins in non-assisted regions in proportion to the non-assisted regions' shares of moves to the four development area regions.

(iii) The remaining job losses not associated with movement have been allocated to non-development area regions in proportion to the size of their manufacturing sectors.

The methods used to estimate the influence of urban structure and regional policy include any multiplier effect within the manufacturing sector. A multiplier of 1.3 has been added to the estimates for industrial structure and size structure to take account of their second-round effects on manufacturing in each region.

2. Employment Accounts for Manufacturing: Cleveland and Leicestershire (Table 8.3)

(a) *Net employment change*

Cleveland: employment change shown by establishment records.

Leicestershire: employment change shown by Department of Employment ER II records, standardised for discontinuities in methods of compilation, etc. The boundaries differ slightly from the administrative county.

(b) *Industrial structure*

Cleveland: structural component of a shift-share analysis using 1965 as the base year and MLH level of disaggregation. Leicestershire: structural component of a shift-share analysis between 1966 and 1975 for the Leicester sub-region (which excludes Melton Mowbray and Oakham) using 1959 as the base year and disaggregating manufacturing into 99 industries.

(c) *Urban structure*

Both counties are dominated by free standing cities. The influence of urban structure is measured by the average differential shift in free standing cities between 1966 and 1975, calculated by a shift-share analysis using 1959 as the base year and disaggregating manufacturing into 99 industries. However, Cleveland is exceptional in that such a high proportion of its manufacturing employment is in steel and heavy chemicals, which do not operate on intra-urban sites and do not experience the constraints normally associated with urban locations. It has been assumed that only 50 per cent of Cleveland's manufacturing employment is in industries which experience urban-rural shifts. This reduces the gain in Cleveland which can be attributed to urban structure.

(d) *Size structure*

Rates of new-firm formation vary according to the size structure of existing manufacturing plants in an area. In Leicestershire the contribution of new and young firms (the total new-firm effect) is measured by establishment records. In Cleveland employment in new firms opening during the period is measured by establishment records, and has been revised upwards by 40 per cent to allow for the growth of young firms. This revision is based upon the ratio between employment growth in young firms and employment in new firms during 1968–75 shown by the Leicestershire data. The U.K. figure against which Cleveland and Leicestershire are compared is calculated using the relationship between large plant domination and rates of new-firm formation (Figure 6.2)

(e) *Regional policy*

Chapter 7 showed that the employment in moves to the development area regions is roughly equivalent to the overall policy effect. Moves out of Leicestershire and moves into

Cleveland are therefore used as a proxy for the impact of regional policy. This should not be taken to imply that all moves are attributable to policy, or that there has been no policy impact on indigenous industry.

References

Allaman, P. A. and Birch, D. L. 1975, *Components of Employment Change for States by Industry Group*, Harvard University-Massachusetts Institute of Technology Joint Centre for Urban Studies, working paper no. 5, Cambridge, Mass.

Allen, K. and Yuill, D. 1978, *Small Area Employment Forecasting: Data and Problems*, Farnborough, Saxon House.

Ashcroft, B. and Taylor, J. 1979, 'The effect of regional policy on the movement of industry in Great Britain' in D. Maclennan and J. B. Parr *(eds.), Regional Policy: Past Experiences and New Directions*, Oxford, Martin Robertson, pp. 43–64.

Atkins, D. H. W. 1973, 'Employment change in branch and parent manufacturing plants in the U.K.: 1966–71', *Trade and Industry*, 30 August, pp. 437–9.

Birch, D. L. 1979, *The Job Generation Process*, M.I.T. Program on Neighbourhood and Regional Change, Cambridge, Mass.

Brown, A. J. 1972, *The Framework of Regional Economics in the United Kingdom*, Cambridge, C.U.P.

Cambridge Economic Policy Group 1980a, *Cambridge Economic Policy Review*, vol. 6, no. 1, Farnborough, Gower.

Cambridge Economic Policy Group 1980b, *Cambridge Economic Policy Review*, vol. 6, no. 2, Farnborough, Gower.

Centre for Interfirm Comparison 1977, *Management Policies and Practices, and Business Performance*, Centre for Interfirm Comparison, Colchester.

Dahmen, E. 1970, *Entrepreneurial Activity and The Development of Swedish Industry*, Homewood, Illinois, Irwin.

Dennis, R. 1978, 'The decline of manufacturing employment in Greater London 1966–74', *Urban Studies*, vol. 15, pp. 63–73.

Department of Industry 1980, *Provision of Small Industrial Premises*, London.

Department of Trade and Industry 1973, Memorandum on the inquiry into location attitudes and experience, *Minutes of Evidence*, Trade and Industry sub-committee of the House of Commons Expenditure Committee, Session 1972–3, pp. 525–668, London, HMSO.

Firn, J. R. and Swales, J. K. 1978, 'The formation of new manufacturing establishments in Central Clydeside and West Midlands conurbations 1963–72: a comparative analysis', *Regional Studies*, vol. 12, pp. 199–213.

Fothergill, S. and Gudgin, G. 1978, *Regional Employment Statistics on a Comparable Basis 1952–75*, Centre for Environmental Studies occasional paper no. 5, London, CES.

Fothergill, S. and Gudgin, G. 1979a, 'Regional employment change: a sub-regional explanation', *Progress in Planning*, vol. 12, pp. 155–219.

Fothergill, S. and Gudgin, G. 1979b, 'In defence of shift-share', *Urban Studies*, vol. 16, pp. 309–19.

Fothergill, S. and Gudgin, G. 1979c, *The Job Generation Process in Britain*, Centre for Environmental Studies research series no. 32, London, CES.

Fraser of Allander Institute, University of Strathclyde 1978, *Input-Output*

Tables for Scotland 1973, Edinburgh, Scottish Academic Press.
Gudgin, G. 1978, *Industrial Location Processes and Regional Employment Growth*, Farnborough, Saxon House.
Howard, R. S. 1968, *The Movement of Manufacturing Industry in the United Kingdom 1945–65*, London, HMSO for the Board of Trade.
Johnson, P. S. and Cathcart, D. 1979, 'The founders of new manufacturing firms: a note on the size of incubator plants', *Journal of Industrial Economics*, vol. 28, pp. 219–24.
JURUE 1979, *Industrial Renewal in The Inner City: An Assessment of Potential and Problems*, Joint Unit for Research on the Urban Environment, University of Aston in Birmingham.
Keeble, D. 1976, *Industrial Location and Planning in The United Kingdom*, London, Methuen.
Keeble, D. 1980, 'Industrial decline, regional policy and the urban-rural manufacturing shift in the United Kingdom', *Environment and Planning A*, vol. 12, pp. 945–62.
Lloyd, P. E. and Dicken, P. 1979, *New Firms, Small Firms and Job Generation: the Experience of Manchester and Meseyside 1966–1975* North West Industry Research Unit working paper no. 9, Manchester, School of Geography.
McCallum, J. D. 1979, 'The development of British regional policy' in D. Maclennan and J. B. Parr (eds.), *Regional Policy: Past Experiences and New Directions*, Oxford, Martin Robertson, pp. 3–41.
MacKay, R. R. and Thomson, L. 1979, 'Important trends in regional policy and regional employment: a modified interpretation', *Scottish Journal of Political Economy*, vol. 26, pp. 233–60.
Merret Cyriax Assocs. 1972, *Dynamics of Small Firms*, Research report no. 12. Committee of Inquiry on Small Firms, London, HMSO.
Moore, B. C. and Rhodes, J. 1973, 'Evaluating the effects of British regional economic policy', *Economic Journal*, vol. 83, pp. 87–110.
Moore, B. C. and Rhodes, J. 1976, 'Regional economic policy and the movement of manufacturing firms to development areas', *Economica*, vol. 43, pp. 17–31.
Moore, B. C., Rhodes, J. and Tyler, P. 1977, 'The impact of regional policy in the 1970s', *Centre for Environmental Studies Review*, no. 1, pp. 67–77.
Moore, B. C., Rhodes, J. and Tyler, P. 1980, *New Developments in the Evaluation of Regional Policy*, paper presented at an SSRC urban and regional economics conference, Birmingham, May 1980.
NEDO 1975, *Financial Tables for The Clothing Industry 1973–74*, London, National Economic Development Office.
NEDO 1975, *Company Financial Results 1970/71–1974/75: Mechanical Engineering EDC*, London, National Economic Development Office.
Richardson, H. W. 1978, *Urban and Regional Economics*, Harmondsworth, Penguin Books.
Robinson, J. F. F. and Storey, D. J. 1981, 'Manufacturing employment change in Cleveland 1965–76', *Regional Studies* (forthcoming).
Smith, C. T. B., Clifton, R., Makeham, P., Creigh, S. W. and Burn, R. V. 1978, *Strikes in Britain*, London, HMSO for the Department of Employment.
Smith, N. R. 1967, *The Entrepreneur and His Firm*, Bureau of Business and Economic Research, University of Michigan, Michigan, Illinois.
Townroe, P. M. 1979, *Industrial Movement: Experience in the U.S. and the U.K.* Farnborough, Saxon House.

Author Index

Subject Index

HAROLD BRIDGES LIBRARY
S. MARTIN'S COLLEGE
LANCASTER